A Special Issue of
the
*European Journal of Developmental Psychology*

# Social cognition in adolescence: A tribute to Sandy (A.E.) Jackson (1937-2003)

Edited by

## Willem Koops
*Utrecht University, The Netherlands*

and

## Harke A. Bosma
*University of Groningen, The Netherlands*

Psychology Press
Taylor & Francis Group
HOVE AND NEW YORK

T0347566

Published in 2004 by Psychology Press Ltd
27 Church Road, Hove, East Sussex, BN3 2FA

Simultaneously published in the USA and Canada
by Psychology Press Ltd
711 Third Avenue, New York, NY 10017

First issued in paperback 2015

*Psychology Press is an imprint of the Taylor and Francis Group, an informa business*

*British Library Cataloguing in Publication Data*
A catalogue record for this book is available from the British Library

ISBN 13: 978-1-138-87324-7 (pbk)
ISBN 13: 978-1-8416-9988-2 (hbk)

ISSN 1740-5629

Cover design by Jim Wilkie
Typeset in the UK by Elite Typesetting Techniques Ltd., Eastleigh, Hampshire

# Contents*

*This book is also a special issue of the journal *European Journal of Developmental Psychology*, and forms issue 4 of Volume 1 (2004). The page numbers are taken from the journal and so begin with p. 281.

EUROPEAN JOURNAL OF DEVELOPMENTAL PSYCHOLOGY, 2004, 1(4), 281–288

# Social cognition in adolescence: A tribute to Sandy (A. E.) Jackson (1937–2003)

Harke A. Bosma
*University of Groningen, The Netherlands*

Willem Koops
*Utrecht University, The Netherlands*

## INTRODUCTION

A complex of biological, cognitive and social changes characterizes the period of adolescence. All these changes affect and are affected by changes in young people's social relations. Their relationships with parents become more symmetrical and the adolescents gain greater freedom to make their own decisions about their behaviour and personal commitments. At the same time relationships with peers become more significant. Within the context of all these changes adolescents may experiment with different roles, forms of relationships and ways of defining and presenting themselves to others. This experimentation can be seen as an essential part of achieving a sense of identity and committing oneself to adult roles and responsibilities. Several factors probably influence the course and outcome of this process. For example: earlier child-rearing experiences, negative as well as positive; the timing and social response to pubertal maturation; critical life events; or negative social learning experiences, leading to inadequate coping and social skills. In interaction with proximal and distal contextual factors (family, peers, school, the neighbourhood, labour market conditions), positive and negative pathways of social development emerge and develop further.

Address correspondence to Harke A. Bosma, Department of Developmental Psychology, University of Groningen, Grote Kruisstraat 2/1, 9712 TS Groningen, The Netherlands. E-mail: H.A.Bosma@ppsw.rug.nl

This Special Issue is based on the papers presented at a workshop which was organized in June 2002 at the retirement of Dr Alexander (Sandy) E. Jackson. This workshop was made possible with grants of the Dutch Science Foundation (NWO), the Psychology Department of the University of Groningen, the Dutch Institute for Research of Education and Development (ISED) and the European Association for Research on Adolescence (EARA).

http://www.tandf.co.uk/journals/pp/17405629.html DOI: 10.1080/17405620444000256

Although a lot of research has been conducted in several of these areas, the role of the individual's social cognitive processes is largely unexplored. In Sandy Jackson's opinion this was remarkable in the face of the varied social problems and negative outcomes of social development, such as ongoing difficulties in relationships with parents, teachers, and authority figures, engagement in abusive or antisocial behaviour, and problems in peer relations and social isolation. Jackson was convinced that further knowledge of the processes and patterns of social development in adolescence could help to understand development and problems in related domains such as identity formation, friendship choice, school and subsequent career development. Furthermore, evidence from adult studies in personality and social psychology has demonstrated the importance of processes like person perception, impression formation, attributions, and stereotyping for ways of relating to others. It could well be that these processes emerge and crystallize in adolescence. Although the continuity of social behaviour between adolescence and adulthood remains to be empirically demonstrated, the lack of research on social cognitive processes and development in adolescence is a principal restraint in the longitudinal assessment of such continuities. Jackson saw this deficiency also as a very serious limitation for the construction of effective forms of intervention in the social development of adolescents.

To illustrate his interest in this area, Jackson often shared the observation that "teenage youngsters in a residential school were prepared to make judgements about a new arrival, whom they had never previously seen, solely on the basis of observing him walk the short distance from the front gate to the school office. In some cases, these same teenagers had been placed in the residential school, having attacked a stranger in the street— simply because they did not like the look of him!" (in Jackson, 1987, p. 24). He made this observation while he was working as a clinical psychologist in a residential setting. When he became a faculty member at the department of Developmental Psychology at Groningen, in 1977, this and similar observations inspired him to start a research program with person perception, impression formation, and the formation of cognitive schemata or scripts in adolescents' social interactions as its key elements. On the basis of four experiments Jackson (1987) could demonstrate how young adolescents ( > 12 years of age) can provide a great deal of psychological information (in the form of interpersonal constructs) about a stranger whom they have only met for a short time in a group situation. Young adolescents, according to these results, have already acquired a set of interpersonal constructs, which they employ in their self-perception and in the perception of friends, acquaintances and people whom they meet for the first time. In these experiments he successfully combined experimental methods with his favoured clinical measure, Kelly's Repertory Grid Technique.

Unfortunately Jackson never took the time to publish the results of this set of experiments in a series of journal articles. They did inspire him, however, to the elaboration of an analytic framework of social interaction sequences for further research into the adolescent's understanding of and participation in the social world. In this framework Jackson (1993) strongly emphasized the role of information processing in the adolescent's social activities. It was his strong conviction that the detailing of these processes could help to describe and understand social thinking in adolescent development. A nice empirical example of such an approach can be found in a publication on the cognitive strategies employed by adolescents in trying to arrange a first date (Jackson, Jacob, Landman-Peeters, & Lanting, 2001). This focus on the adolescents' cognitive construction of their social worlds can also be found in other publications by Jackson and colleagues (e.g., Jackson & Rodriguez-Tomé, 1993; Jackson, Cicognani, & Charman, 1996; Jackson, Bijstra, Oostra, & Bosma, 1998). Given his clinical background and his interest in developmental psychopathology, Jackson also tried to always link his teaching and research to applied questions. His dissertational research already showed how he used fundamental research to answer questions that came up in his clinical work. In relation to his social-cognitive orientation he showed a strong interest in social skills training and the effect of interventions in adolescent social development (Bijstra, Bosma, & Jackson, 1994; Bijstra, Jackson, & Bosma, 1995; Jackson & Bijstra, 2000).

Sandy Jackson's contributions to developmental psychology comprise his interconnected clinical and scientific experiences and publications. His enthusiasm and his warm, outgoing style of interaction with colleagues all over the world made him also a leader in boosting the internationalizing of adolescence psychology and developmental psychology at large, particularly at the European level. He was the founder and first president of the European Association for Research on Adolescence (EARA) and he was—together with the late George Butterworth—the founder of the European Society for Developmental Psychology (ESDP) as well as the cofounder (together with Michel Deleau and Willem Koops) of its flagship journal, the *European Journal of Developmental Psychology*. Sandy Jackson retired in June 2002, and an international workshop was organized to wrap up the impact of his work. Now, this special issue is simply the publication of the contributions to this symposium. Sandy was not able to edit this volume—he suffered for many years from cancer and in the summer of 2003 he passed away among his family in his beloved Scotland. As editors, we have tried to make the issue as good as Sandy would have liked it to be.

The papers presented at the original workshop, and the articles in this special issue, reflect the main themes in Jackson's work:

- First, what scientific progress has been made with regard to the study of fundamental processes and developmental pathways in social cognitive development in adolescence? (Articles by Mascolo & Margolis; and Berzonsky.)
- Second, how is social cognitive development related to other areas of development in adolescence? (Articles by Persson, Stattin, & Kerr; Van Aken & Dubas; and Honess.)
- And, finally, how effective are interventions in social cognitive development in adolescence? (Articles by Seiffge-Krenke; Kurtines et al.; and Lichtwarck-Aschoff & Van Geert.)

## Social cognitive development in adolescence: Recent theoretical approaches

In the first article, entitled "Social cognition as a mediator in adolescent development: A coactive systems approach" Mascolo and Margolis see social knowledge as a set of dynamic representations that arise and function in on-line action and social interaction, thus as emerging from co-regulated social interactions. This knowledge does not occur independently from other psychological processes—it comprises the mutual regulation of appraisal, affect and action. Mascolo and Margolis' elaboration of a dynamic developmental theory of adolescent social-cognitive development follows Kurt Fischer's (neo-Piagetian) theory of the development of cognitive skills. Skills are actions on (social) objects, and are tied to specific domains and tasks within these domains. Skilled action develops in multiple trajectories both within and between persons ("the developmental web" as a metaphor). This approach is illustrated with data on the development of responsive, dominating and avoidant interaction strategies and an example of social meaning making in co-regulated social interactions.

In the second article, entitled "Identity processing styles, self-construction, and personal epistemic assumptions: A social-cognitive perspective", Berzonsky defines identity as a self-theory, a cognitive structure that "directs and governs the processes and resources adolescents use to cope and adapt in everyday life". Its development involves "an ongoing, dialectical interchange between assimilative processes governed by the identity structure and accommodative processes directed by the social and physical contexts within which adolescents live and develop". Adolescents differ in how they deal with the tasks of maintaining and revising their sense of identity. These differences can be assessed with Berzonsky's identity style measure, which comprises an informational, a normative and a diffuse/avoidant orientation in the processing of identity-relevant information. Empirical research has confirmed the predicted relationships of the styles with other identity processes (exploration and commitment), coping strategies (functional versus dysfunctional), cognitive strategies (Epstein: intuitive and rational processing). In summary, this body of research suggests that adolescents who differ in their predominant use of identity style also show clear differences in the flexibility and adaptability of their identity structure, in other words, can be seen as different types of self-theorists—informational types are most likely to engage in rational processing of identity relevant information, while normative types will show an assimilative bias and diffuse/avoidant types an accommodative bias.

## Social cognitive development in adolescence and its relationship to other core developmental processes

The third article is authored by Persson, Stattin and Kerr and its title is "Adolescents' conceptions of family democracy: Does their own behaviour play a role?" The designs of studies of family democracy are almost always correlational, but conclusions tend to be phrased in terms of parents *affecting* their adolescent offspring. In general, parenting research fails to see adolescents as active agents in parent–adolescent interactions. In this empirical study about 1100 adolescents answered a questionnaire comprising several measures. They were asked among other things to compare their family to a country and their parents to its leaders and to indicate what type of government they had: a democracy; a dictatorship; an anarchy; or a country where a revolution had taken place. Parents' warmth appears to be a strong predictor of family democracy. When controlling for perceived parents' behaviour adolescents' openness to communication adds significantly to a democratic family climate. Both parties, thus actively contribute to the democracy in the family.

The fourth article, by Van Aken and Dubas, is entitled "Personality type, social relationships, and problem behaviour in adolescence". It focuses on the transactions between the adolescents' personality organization and their social relationships with parents and peers. Data of a three-year longitudinal study of about 560 adolescents (measured each year, about 12 to 15 years of age at the first measurement) are used to: (1) study the change and stability of the three repeatedly found personality types (resilient, overcontrolled, and undercontrolled), the psychosocial functioning of each type (internalizing, externalizing and social problems); and (2) how the quality of their relationships and parental coercion is related these types, their longitudinal changes and functioning. Type membership appears to be moderately stable. The resilients show most favourable relationships and lowest levels of coercion; the overcontrollers report low support, more internalizing and social problems, the undercontrollers low support and most coercion and more internalizing, social, and externalizing problems. The interactions between personality type and support predict problem behaviour, the causal directions, however, are not yet clear.

The fifth article is entitled "Family judgements about adolescent problems: Where respondents overlap and why they disagree". In this empirical study, Honess investigates the variation between different family members' appraisals of adolescent adjustment. His method leads him to examine mothers; fathers and adolescents in 50 families, using individual interviews and ratings with the help of the Achenbach check lists. Variation is partly explained by relating these to the concerns each family member expresses about the adolescent's future. Parents appear to operate within a distinct subsystem in talking about concerns and adjustment problems in comparison to their adolescent child. In particular, the parents' concerns about their child's poor attitude appear to drive their assessment of adjustment difficulties; whereas the adolescent appears to be more influenced by concerns about personal relationships outside of the family system. Participants did, however, demonstrate awareness of others' concerns. In social-cognitive terms, appraisals are context sensitive and appear to reflect different criteria for what constitutes social competence.

## Social cognitive development in adolescence: Does intervention change anything?

In the sixth article entitled "Adaptive and maladaptive coping styles: Does intervention change anything?" Seiffge-Krenke focuses on coping as a core process, which is linked to current and future social functioning in adolescence. Adolescents show enormous gains in social-cognitive skills. Most of them can competently solve conflicts and cope with everyday stressors. The increased differentiation and maturity in coping skills is another sign of the adolescent growth in social-cognitive competence. Cognition (appraisal) plays a central role in coping. Adolescents use active support-seeking and internal reflection of possible solutions much more often than denial or withdrawal strategies (respectively 45%, 35%, and 20%). Avoidant coping is a clear risk factor. It is strongly related to a maladaptive pathway through adolescence. Such a pathway can lead from bad to worse: "The accumulation of stressors, a dysfunctional coping style, and deficits in relationships create a vicious circle, thus contributing to increased symptomatology". Can intervention change anything? Yes, for those adolescents who remain in treatment. Drop out rates are high, though. Therapy is more effective for internalizing than externalizing problems. Interventions with peer support groups can be quite effective, unless the peers have antisocial problems or are depressed. In that case the intervention becomes a "deviancy training", which increases problem behaviour.

In the seventh article Kurtines, Montgomery, Lewis Arango, and Kortsch report their work on "New directions in promoting positive youth development". In the literature several programs have been reported that successfully reduce adolescent behaviour problems or reduce risk factors and increase protective factors. Recently there is a growing literature on programs that seek to promote positive development. The Changing Lives Program at Florida International University is such a program. It tries "to promote positive qualitative change in participants' lives in ways that are individually, culturally, historically, and developmentally meaningful and significant". Documenting and evaluating these type of programs, however, is very complex and difficult. They lack the specificity of treatment and intervention programs. To do this, Kurtines and colleagues developed a methodological framework that comprises as a core cycle: (1) the coding of qualitative data into categories; (2) the identification of theoretically plausible patterns in the identified categories; (3) the generation of hypotheses, based on the patterns; and (4) the quantitative analysis and testing of hypotheses. Two pilot studies are presented to illustrate the application of this framework in the evaluation of the effects of their Changing Lives Program. The results nicely demonstrate the usefulness of integrating qualitative and quantitative methods.

The last article in this special issue is by Lichtwarck-Aschoff and Van Geert. Its title is "A dynamic systems perspective on social cognition, problematic behaviour and intervention in adolescence". After a short and compact exposition of their dynamic systems perspective on social cognition and behaviour, the authors come to the following central question in their article: "Why has the same intervention varying results for different individuals?" They assert that a dynamic systems approach will interpret these varying results as meaningful variation (instead of as error variance) and thus have the capacity to study and evaluate the process of intervention in all its complexity. They argue that the traditional recommendation of the random control group design for the study of the effects of interventions is not warranted.

## CONCLUSION

This series of papers highlights the preoccupations of Sandy Jackson, which at the same time are major issues of present-day adolescence research. In the concluding discussion, the participants of the original workshop focused on the question how "social cognition" is construed and brought into our adolescent research. Two perspectives emerge. One position can easily be characterized by the statement that "all cognition is social"—from this perspective social cognition permeates all the work presented at the workshop and in this special issue. Is it actually an umbrella concept? Participants who favour the other position (as Sandy Jackson did) argue that social cognition should be defined much more specifically. It then refers to literatures such as the social-psychological literature on biases in self-perception, and the developmental traditions on perspective taking and the child's theory of mind. From this perspective, isn't there a gap in our knowledge? For example, on how social cognition develops in adolescence, and which factors and processes are involved?

We simply cannot say that the papers in the workshop, published in this special issue, provide final answers to these questions, but we can say that over a long period, past, present, and future, these Jacksonian issues have remained and will remain among us, motivating and stimulating our theoretical discussions. And so will, in our memory, our friend and colleague, Sandy Jackson.

# REFERENCES

Bijstra, J. O., Bosma, H. A., & Jackson, S. [A. E.] (1994). The relationship between social skills and psycho-social functioning in early adolescence. *Personality and Individual Differences, 16*, 767–776.

Bijstra, J.O., Jackson, S. [A. E.], & Bosma, H. A. (1995). Social skills and psychosocial functioning in early adolescence: A three-year follow-up. *International Journal of Adolescent Medicine & Health, 8*, 221–233.

Jackson, A. E. (1987). *Perceptions of a new acquaintance in adolescence.* Groningen, The Netherlands: Stichting Kinderstudies.

Jackson, A. E. (1993). Social behaviour in adolescence: The analysis of social interaction sequences. In S. [A. E.] Jackson & H. Rodriguez-Tomé (Eds.), *The social worlds of adolescence* (pp. 15–45). Hove, UK: Lawrence Erlbaum Associates Ltd.

Jackson, S. [A. E.],, & Bijstra, J. O. (2000). Overcoming psychosocial difficulties in adolescence: Toward the development of social competence. *European Review of Applied Psychology, 50*, 267–274.

Jackson, S. [A. E.], Bijstra, J. O., Oostra, L., & Bosma, H. A. (1998). Adolescents' perceptions of communication with parents relative to specific aspects of relationships with parents and personal development. *Journal of Adolescence, 21*, 305–322.

Jackson, S. [A. E.], Cicognani, E., & Charman, L. (1996). The measurement of conflict in parent–adolescent relationships. In L. Verhofstadt-Denève, I. Kienhorst, & C. Braet (Eds.), *Conflict and development in adolescence* (pp. 75–91). Leiden, The Netherlands: DSWO Press, Leiden University.

Jackson, S. [A. E.], Jacob, M. N., Landman-Peeters, K., & Lanting, A. (2001). Cognitive strategies employed in trying to arrange a first date. *Journal of Adolescence, 24*, 267–279.

Jackson, S. [A. E.], & Rodriguez-Tomé, H. (Eds.). (1993). *The social worlds of adolescence.* Hove, UK: Lawrence Erlbaum Associates Ltd.

EUROPEAN JOURNAL OF DEVELOPMENTAL PSYCHOLOGY, 2004, *1*(4), 289–302

# Social cognition as a mediator of adolescent development: A coactive systems approach

Michael F. Mascolo and Deborah Margolis

*Merrimack College, North Andover, USA*

The study of social cognition often follows as an attempt to represent the structure and content of social knowledge assumed to be located within individual social actors. While we have learned much from the study of social cognition, traditional approaches maintain a sharp distinction between cognition and action. As such, they raise the question of how inner knowledge becomes translated into social action. An alternative approach proceeds by studying social cognition *in medias res*—in the middle of everything (Fischer & Bidell, 1998). From this view, social cognition functions as a form of acting and as a mediator of action and development. In what follows, we elaborate a coactive systems framework for understanding how social meanings develop as mediators of social action in adolescence.

## A COACTIVE SYSTEMS CONCEPTION OF SOCIAL ACTION

Figure 1 provides a schematic representation of the coactive person–environment system. From this view, the person–environment system is composed of five basic classes of elements: within a given *sociocultural context*, individual *action* is directed toward physical or psychological *objects*. In social interaction, individuals engage dialogically with other *persons* through the use of *mediational means* (e.g., cultural tools). A coactive systems conception maintains that action and experience is the coactive product of relations among evolving elements of the system (Fischer & Bidell, 1998; Gottlieb, Wahlsten, & Lickliter, 1998; Lewis & Granic, 2000; Mascolo, 2004a; Mascolo & Fischer, 1998, in press; Oyama, 2000). As such, human action is the emergent product of coactive *relations among elements* of the system rather than the outcome of particular elements considered separately.

---

Address correspondence to Michael F. Mascolo, Merrimack College, North Andover, MA 01845, USA. E-mail: Michael_Mascolo@yahoo.com

http://www.tandf.co.uk/journals/pp/17405629.html        DOI: 10.1080/17405620444000256

**The Person-Environment System**

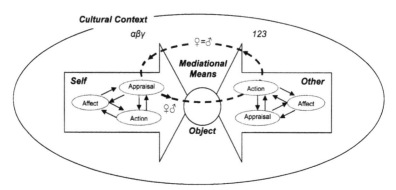

**Figure 1.** The co-active person–environment system. The large arrows indicate that individual action is directed toward physical or symbolic objects and is composed of integrations of component processes. The circular arrow indicates that mediational means (signs, cultural tools) are appropriated from culture; transform individual and joint action; and can themselves be transformed and reinserted anew into the cultural systems from which they were culled.

Mutual regulation of psychological processes occurs both between and within individuals. Between persons, interpersonal communication is mediated through the use of cultural tools, most notably signs and symbols (Wertsch, 1998). In so doing, social partners use meanings that are represented sign systems to mediate their interactions (Cole, 1996; Mascolo, 2004b; Vygotsky, 1978; Wertsch, 1998). As such, in development, to acquire facility with language is to gain access to cultural meanings shared by a linguistic community. Within individuals, we differentiate between three broad categories of psychological processes: *appraisal*; *affect*; and *muscle action*. *Appraisal processes* refer to assessments of relations between perceived events and one's goals, motives and concerns (Mascolo, Fischer, & Li, 2003). Affective processes refer to feeling-producing processes. Muscle actions result in changes both internal and external to the person. As depicted in Figure 1, the dual arrows between appraisal, affective and action components signify co-regulation. For example, as appraisals modulate affect, affect simultaneously provides feedback that *selects, amplifies* and *organizes* appraisal processes. Changes in feeling tone take place as appraisal systems detect differences in the fate of a person's goals, motives and concerns.

In this way, a fully coactive account of the role of social cognition in adolescent development would proceed as an attempt to articulate the structure and content of *contextualized* social meanings that are and *integrated with affect, motivation, and other psychological systems.* Such an approach would focus on identifying dynamic and integrative structures in meaning-in-action rather than static, abstract and decontextualized stages of social-cognitive understanding.

## THE DEVELOPMENT OF SOCIAL MEANING-MAKING IN ADOLESCENCE

Drawing upon an elegant review and theoretical analysis by Rubin, Bukowski and Parker (1998), Table 1 provides a descriptive account of the types of peer interactions often evinced by many children regarded as *popular, aggressive-rejected* and *withdrawn-rejected* in Western European and North American culture, as well as the developmental processes that mediate such developmental outcomes. According to Rubin, Bukowski and Parker (1998), relative to other sociometric status groupings, children who are regarded as *popular* are able to size up the consensual meanings that define a given social situation, and to proactively but not disruptively position themselves within those meanings (Newcomb, Bukowski, & Pattee, 1993). In this way, popular children seem able to achieve their personal goals while simultaneously maintaining positive relations with interlocutors.

TABLE 1
Origins of peer interaction styles in popular, rejected and neglected children

| | *Popular* | *Rejected-aggressive* | *Rejected-withdrawn* |
|---|---|---|---|
| *Peer relation strategies* | • Reads social frames<br>• Reads other's perspective | • Difficulty with social frames<br>• Misattributes intentions | • Withdraws from social interaction<br>• Avoids conflict |
| | • Assert personal goals while preserving friendship | • Hostile assertion of personal goals | • Submits to other's agenda |
| *Emotional-relational bias* | • Positive emotional bias<br>• High cognitive Control<br>• "Easy" temperament<br>• Capacity for empathy | • Negative emotion bias<br>• Anger affective organization<br>• Low cognitive control<br>• "Difficult" temperament | • Behavioural inhibition<br>• Wariness-fear affective organization |
| *Social-relational history* | • Secure attachment<br>• Authoritative or harmonious parenting<br>• Affective sharing and attunement in peer relations | • Socialization agents experience difficulty with socio-emotional regulation<br>• Rejection by peers<br>• Absence of co-operative relations with peers | • Socialization agents experience difficulty introducing novelty<br>• Difficulty entering into peer relations<br>• Lack of experience with peers |

Rubin, Bukowski and Parker (1998) differentiate two classes of rejected children: *aggressive-rejected* and *withdrawn-rejected*. The most frequently cited indicator of peer rejection is *aggression* (Bukowski & Newcomb, 1984; Dodge, 1983). However, all rejected children are not viewed as aggressive; nor are all aggressive children rejected. Children exhibiting aggressive tendencies comprise only 40 – 50% of rejected children (Rubin et al., 1998). Approximately 10 – 20% of rejected children exhibit propensities toward excessive social withdrawal. Researchers have categorized this group as *rejected-withdrawn*. Of course, not all socially withdrawn children are rejected; only 25% of children exhibiting social withdrawal become rejected (Rubin, Bukowski, & Parker, 1998).

## PATHWAYS IN THE DEVELOPMENT OF PEER INTERACTION SKILLS

Rubin, Bukowski and Parker (1998) state: "Acceptance by peers is largely a function of the child's social skills; in normal circumstances, all else is secondary" (p. 677). In this section, we first outline a model of skill development that allows precise identification of the structure and developmental pathways of social action and thought (Fischer & Bidell, 1998). Thereafter, using this model, we propose alternative pathways in the development of social skills used by socially successful, rejected-aggressive, rejected-avoidant children and adolescents.

### The dynamics of developing social skills

Dynamic skill theory (Fischer, 1980; Fischer & Bidell, 1998; Mascolo & Fischer, 1998) provides a set of conceptual and methodological tools for charting transformations in the skills that mediate social action over the course of adolescence. The central unit in dynamic skill theory is the *skill*—a capacity to organize actions, thoughts, and feelings within a given context for a specific goal or task. Skilled action varies dynamically as a function of temperament, emotional state, task demands, social relationship, culture, and other such conditions. As such, skills are not internal competencies or properties of a child per se; instead, they are properties of a child-in-a-social-context. Skill theory defines a developmental scale and a series of rules and methods for analysing developing thought and action. The scale consists of 13 developmental levels grouped into four broad *tiers* from birth through adulthood: (1) *reflexes* (innate action components, emerging shortly after birth); (2) *sensori-motor actions* (controlled actions on objects, emerging around four months); (3) *representations* (concrete symbolic meanings, 18 – 24 months); and (4) *abstractions* (generalized and intangible meanings, 11 – 12 years). Within each tier, skills pass through four levels: *single sets; mappings; systems;* and *systems of systems.* The last level within a tier—systems of systems—constitutes the first level of the next broad developmental tier.

Skills develop as children co-ordinate lower-level actions into higher-order wholes within particular tasks, conceptual domains, and social contexts. Individuals are able to function at higher levels in contexts that provide high rather than low levels of social support (Fischer, Bullock, Rotenberg, & Raya, 1993; Rogoff, 2003; Vygotsky, 1978). Two important implications follow from these points. First, one can specify a *developmental range* that describes the distance between an individual's functional level of activity in unsupportive contexts and one's optimal level of performance in more supportive contexts (Fischer et al., 1993). Second, development is like a *web* with alternative and interconnected pathways, rather than a ladder using a single, unidirectional sequence of steps (Fischer & Bidell, 1998). Figure 2 depicts three ways that developing social skills exhibit dynamic variation between and within individual children. First, individual strands in the developmental web can represent pathways along which various skills develop within individual children. Second, within individual children, the *developmental range itself* can vary depending upon the target skill domain. A child may exhibit a different range of skill for enacting responsive strategies than for constructing avoidant or aggressive strategies. Finally, there are individual differences in the *pattern of developmental ranges* that children from different sociometric groupings exhibit across skill domains.

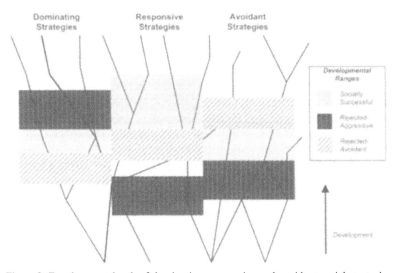

**Figure 2.** Developmental web of dominating, responsive and avoidant social strategies.

## Alternative trajectories in the development of social interaction skills

We propose three overlapping, yet partially distinct, pathways in the development of social skills from childhood through adolescence. These include the *responsive, dominant-aggressive* and *avoidant-submissive* pathways. Responsive interaction skills reflect an individual's capacity to sustain personal and social goals in a social situation while preserving the relationship between self and other (Rubin & Rose-Krasnor, 1992). *Dominant-aggressive* interactive skills refer to the use of power or force to bring about personal and social goals with little regard for one's social partner's goals, beliefs and desires. *Avoidant-submissive* interaction skills involve the active avoidance of social interaction, especially under novel conditions, and/or the deferring of one's personal goals to those of others. Although all children exhibit each interactive style from time to time, we suggest that interaction skills for socially successful children are organized largely around the responsive pathway; for rejected-aggressive children around the dominant-aggressive pathway, and for rejected-avoidant children around the avoidant-submissive pathway.

*The development of responsive interaction strategies.* In terms of skill theory (Fischer, 1980), a 6- to 7-year-old child is able to construct concrete *representational systems*. Representational systems begin to emerge around 6–7 years with the capacity to co-ordinate two representational mappings into a flexible yet still concrete thought structure. At this level a child can represent a large number of responsive interaction strategies involving concrete self–other relations. We suggest four: *direct request*; *social gambit*; *identifying commonality*; and *indirect cueing*. At the representational level, *direct request* signifies a line of thought such as: "Karla is playing hopscotch and I want to play too. Maybe if I ask her, she might play with me". Another strategy is *social gambit*, in which a child makes an overture to another child based on an inference about that child's desires: "Jordan seems to like playing hopscotch. Maybe if I tell him I know a new way to play, he might like trying to do it. Then he might let me play". The social gambit differs from the direct request in that it is less direct and less intrusive; it also involves less threat of rejection—if Jordan rejects the offer, he rejects the game, not the self.

*Identifying commonality* represents another indirect way of entering into a play interaction. Based on an inference of the other's ongoing interest, a child can make remarks indicating a common, pleasurable activity: "Brenda seems to like hopscotch; if I tell her that she plays well and show her that I can play too, she might ask me to play too". Like social gambit, this strategy is less risky than the direct request. The least intrusive strategy involves *indirect cueing*, and reflects a line of reasoning such as: "If I stand too close to Zoe, she won't like me. Instead, I'll look at her and then look away. Then maybe she'll ask me to play".

These various acts reflect *responsive* strategies, which allow a child to position his personal goals in relation to the internal states of others and the implicit rules that define the social situation. With entry into adolescence, a child becomes capable of integrating multiple such concrete strategies and meanings into a single abstract representation. With the capacity for abstraction, the adolescent can gain an appreciation for the generalized other, for social relationships, and for her positions within various social groups.

Of course, social interactions are not abstract; they arise in action at the concrete nexus of meaning, affect, context and interlocutor. One can think of the adolescent as constructing and deploying increasingly more encompassing and reflective *theories* of his or her self-in-social-interaction (Harré, 1984; Moshman, 1998). In so doing, individuals abstract over what is common to lower-level strategies and meanings. Such higher-level abstractions then function as top-level reference standards or goals specifying idealized ways of presenting self to others (Carver & Scheier, 2000; Goffman, 1959; Mascolo, Fischer, & Neimeyer, 1999). Thus, rather than reflecting fixed or static inner competences, social abstractions function as dynamic control structures whose instantiation is modulated by the vagaries of affect, interlocutor and context.

Beginning around 10–11 years of age, pre-adolescents gain the capacity to construct single abstractions. At this point, children can begin to construct an abstract awareness of the need for responsivity to group standards, such as "I need to be cool in order to fit in". Such an abstraction can be expressed using a variety of strategies for gaining entry with peer groups. A pre-teen can understand "being cool" in terms of group standards such as being seen at the mall or wearing socially sanctioned clothing. Such an awareness might be expressed in social gambits such as: "Hey, I'm going to the mall alone on Saturday, wanna come?" Beginning around 14–15 years of age, using abstract mappings, adolescents can construct a co-ordinated relationship between two single abstract representations. At this level, adolescents can make more subtle differentiations in their representations of self in relation to group expectations. For example, a middle-adolescent can construct an awareness that "coolness is appearing socially attractive and available to others, but appearing *too* available means that I can't attract friends on my own". With the onset of abstract systems at around 17–18 years, older adolescents and young adults can begin to co-ordinate abstract relations between at least two abstract mappings. An adolescent can represent the need for the self to be both *available* and *assertive* in relation to *generalized group values*, while at the same time *not seeming too interested* or *too intrusive*.

*The development of dominating interaction strategies.* Although we tend to view dominating strategies as maladaptive and contrary to social values, most people invoke dominating (and avoidant) strategies from time to time. In the representational tier of development, even kindergarteners evince a variety of different ineffective dominating social strategies (Packer & Scott, 1992). Six- to seven-year-old children have already begun to develop skill in differentiating when dominating strategies may work to their benefit and when they may not. Using *dominant intrusion*, knowing that a lower status child will not fight back, the self simply demands a turn. Using a *confrontational gambit*, realizing his interlocutor rivals his status or strength, the self may challenge the other. In *protective avoidance*, in interactions with a more popular child, the self may withdraw and devalue the task out of fear of embarrassment. Thus, even within a socioemotional trajectory, there is dynamic variation in strategy choice. A child whose strategies are organized around dominance can assume different positions along a dominating–submissive continuum (Pepler & Craig, 1999; Sroufe & Fleeson, 1986).

During pre-adolescence, dominating children can begin to organize abstract social goals and identities around a dominating or "tough" image. The self can be "overpowering", "tough" or "weak" depending upon his or her interlocutor. With development, single abstractions become increasingly differentiated into abstract mappings: "I can overpower unpopular classmates because they are afraid to fight back"; "My tough friends can resist me so I have to teach them to respect me"; and privately, "I stay away from the popular cliques because they can embarrass and humiliate me". With development, these abstract mappings can be co-ordinated into increasingly integrated abstract systems: "Popular kids can humiliate me; they are stupid anyway so I keep my distance. But most kids aren't as tough as me and they fear me. I can just do what I want when I'm with them or else show them that they can't disrespect me".

*The development of avoidant interaction strategies.* Avoidant interaction strategies are organized around affective states involving fear of embarrassment in social circumstances. Using *avoidance*, a seven-year-old is able to represent his own wishes in relation to another child, nonetheless he fears embarrassment and thus chooses to withdraw from social gaze. Alternatively, fearing embarrassment, a child may choose to hover near others in the hope that they may extend an invitation to play (*avoidant onlooking*). *Avoidant-submission* is most likely to be used in interactions with higher-status children. Feeling that he cannot compete with a popular or overpowering child, a child may simply submit to the other child in an attempt to solicit friendship or positive feelings.

During pre-adolescence, children can begin to construct identities around the abstract social goal of *avoiding embarrassment*. Using abstract mappings, a child can develop a higher-order understanding that: "People in popular cliques can humiliate me just by my being around them; if I defer to the group, I can avoid embarrassment and humiliation". Such models can become still more differentiated and integrated as older adolescents begin to use abstract systems around 18 – 19 years of age. With the capacity to relate two abstract mappings, older adolescents and young adults begin to construct integrated social identities organized around the need to avoid humiliation. For example, co-ordinating two abstract mappings, an 18-year-old can form an abstract system like: "I have some close friends who know me and like me. I can seek them out and feel comfortable being myself. But most cliques, especially the popular kids, intimidate me. I generally keep to myself in order to avoid embarrassment and humiliation".

## The dynamics of social meaning-making in joint action

In co-regulated exchanges, the actions of the other are part of the process of the self's actions. In this way, social meanings that mediate action are themselves shaped within particular affective-charged interactions, relationships and sociocultural contexts. As such, it is important to examine how social meanings arise and operate within particular interactions. Toward this end, we interviewed an 8th grade art teacher in an urban school system serving predominantly Hispanic students in the greater Boston area. We asked the teacher to identify a single aggressive-rejected student in her class, and to describe situations in which this individual had occasion to interact with a: popular child, a rejected-avoidant child, and another aggressive-rejected child. The teacher identified a 13-year-old girl (C) who she described as persistently oppositional in class both to her fellow students and to the teacher.

Figure 3 depicts a series of *relational skill diagrams* (Mascolo, 2004a) that provide representations of the structure of thinking, feeling and acting as they are *distributed between* social partners in three different social interactions. In the relational skill diagram, each individual's sensori-motor-affective state is represented in terms of the presences of indicators of different families of emotion that are expressed in the *face, voice, body* and within *instrumental action*. The symbol depicted between individual skill structures represents the specific form of co-regulation that occurs within the social interaction. The symbol simply indicates which party plays a more dominant role in the interaction. The wide face of the symbol placed between skill individual structures indicates the partner who exhibits dominance.

The top panel of Figure 3 provides a representation of a typical interaction between C and an avoidant-rejected girl (S). In this situation, S is

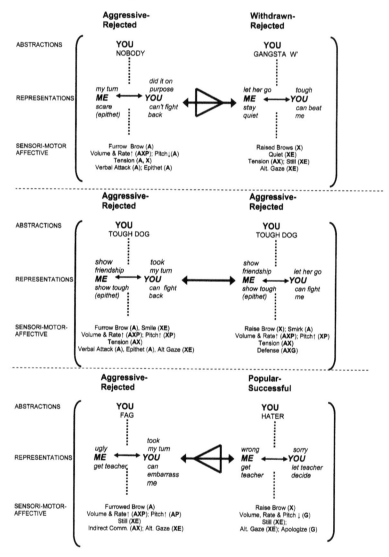

**Figure 3.** The joint production of social positioning in three peer relationships. Each side of each diagram depicts hierarchical control structures for individual social partners organized at the abstract, representational and sensorimotor levels. For the sensorimotor level, capital letters in parentheses identify emotion families associated with indicated acts: anger (A); anxiety (X); embarrassment (E); guilt/sorry (G); and positive affect/affiliation (P).

298

speaking when C wants to gain the floor. At the level of single abstractions, C thinks of S as "a nobody", someone incapable of challenging her status. Using single abstractions, C can formulate a generalized representation like: "I can have my way with Nobodies". These abstractions constrain the deployment of social strategies at the level of concrete representational systems. In one situation, C said: "Sit the fuck down, I'm trying to take a turn". Within this level, guided by her concrete intention to speak, and knowing that S cannot fight back, C formulates a strategy to scare S into backing down. Simultaneously, at the sensorimotor-affective level, C's verbalizations are accompanied by indicators of anger family emotions. In this context, C's interlocutor, S, represents C as a "gansta wannabe" ("gangster want-to-be")—a pejorative term culled from the local peer culture that refers to a child who fancies herself as tough. Using a single abstraction, S can represent a general rule such as: "I can't challenge a gangster wannabe by myself". This abstraction constrains her strategic thinking and action at the level of concrete representations. Thinking: "C will win if I talk back, so I better just stay quiet and let her go". S yields to C exhibiting indicators of anxiety and perhaps embarrassment (e.g., raised brows; controlled stillness; bodily tension, gaze aversion). The important point is that *these relational skill structures illustrate the ways in which structures of social-thought-in-action emerge within co-regulated action that occurs in real time; they are not static properties of individuals considered independently of each other.* The symbol placed in the middle of the relational skill diagram indicates that C dominates the interaction, and S adjusts her behaviour accordingly.

A different pattern of interaction emerges when C interacts with her only friend; a dominating girl who is also rejected (K). In this interaction (depicted in the middle panel of Figure 3), at the level of single abstractions, C and her friend (K) view each other as "tough dawgs". The term "dawg" is used within the peer culture to refer to a "loyal friend". C can construct a generalized abstraction such as: "My dawgs have to respect me". This abstraction constrains the formulation of an interaction strategy at the level of concrete representations. Knowing that K *can* fight back, C intends to take her turn while maintaining both her friendship and her "tough dawg" image. As a result, smiling, and making conciliatory body movements, C says "Sit the fuck down girl, I'm trying to speak". Here, C mixes emotional actions indicating affiliation with indicators of aggression and toughness. In this context, knowing that C can fight back, she yields to her, displaying a simultaneous mix of aggression and affiliation. Smirking with upraised hands and increasing pitch, K says: "Don't get on my grill [back off]! I'm just saying my piece". C's utterance to K is virtually identical to her communication with S, but they are embedded in very different patterns of co-regulated socioemotional exchange.

The bottom panel of Figure 3 displays the structure of an interaction between C and a popular, socially successful girl (V). Relations between these two girls are manifested in stances of mutual disrespect and perhaps fear. At the abstract level, C represents V as a "fag", which is defined in terms of a single abstraction like: "Popular girls are pretty little fags who think they can get whatever they want". Conversely, V views C as a "hater". In the local peer culture, the term "hater" is used to refer to someone who is "annoying because she simply hates other people". V can form an abstraction like: "Haters are just annoying trouble-makers who should be avoided". These abstract social meanings constrain the formation of concrete interaction strategies characterized by anxious avoidance. Both girls look to the teacher in order to solve the conflict. C, attributing purposeful intent to V, feels slighted, and may experience feelings of anger and self-conscious emotion. In an assertive yet anxious tone, C petitions the teacher for help: "She's taking my turn!" Similarly, V also defers to the teacher to solve the problem. In this case, when the teacher asks V to yield the floor, V complies and apologizes with plaintive guilt-like affect. Motivated by different representations of the other, both girls save face (Goffman, 1959) by avoiding each other and deferring to the authority of a third party.

## SOCIAL COGNITION AS EMBEDDED AND EMBODIED MEANING MAKING

We have argued that rather than thinking of social knowledge as a system of structures or processes that lie behind social action, it is more helpful to understand social cognition as a form of *social action* itself. In so doing, we have adopted a stance that might be called *analytic holism*. Human action and experience is composed of multiple subsystems and processes that co-act as a single unified system. We use the term analytic holism to refer to the idea that while it is possible to perform empirical analyses of particular subsystems of action (e.g., perception, emotion, social cognition), it is nonetheless essential to understand how particular subsystems function as a part the activity of the whole individual within its social environment. In so doing, as we approach the study of social cognition, we can come to see not only how social meanings mediate social interaction, but also how such meanings evolve within co-regulated exchanges and local contexts of meaning.

## REFERENCES

Bukowski, W. M. & Newcomb, A. F. (1984). Stability and determinants of sociometric status and friendship choice: A longitudinal perspective. *Developmental Psychology, 20,* 941–952.

Carver, C. S., & Scheier, M. F. (2000). Autonomy and self regulation. *Psychological Inquiry, 11*, 284–291.

Cole, M. (1996). *Cultural psychology: A once and future discipline*. Cambridge, MA: Harvard University Press.

Dodge, K. A. (1983). Behavioral antecedents of peer social status. *Child Development, 54*, 1386–1399.

Fischer, K. (1980). A theory of cognitive development: The control and construction of hierarchies of skills. *Psychological Review, 87*, 477–531.

Fischer, K. W., & Bidell, T. R. (1998). Dynamic development of psychological structures in action and thought. In W. Damon & R. M. Lerner (Eds.), *Handbook of child psychology: Theoretical models of human development* (5th ed., pp. 467–561). New York: Wiley.

Fischer, K. W., Bullock, D., Rotenberg, E. J., & Raya, P. (1993). The dynamics of competence: How context contributes directly to skill. In R. Wozniak & K. W. Fischer (Eds.), *Development in context: Acting and thinking in specific environments* (pp. 93–117). Hillsdale, NJ: Lawrence Erlbaum Associates, Inc.

Goffman, E. (1959). *The presentation of self in everyday life*. New York: Doubleday.

Gottlieb, G., Wahlsten, D., & Lickliter, R. (1998). The significance of biology for human development: A developmental psychobiological systems view. In R. Lerner (Ed.), *Handbook of child psychology: Vol. 1. Theory* (pp. 233–273). New York: Wiley.

Harré, R. (1984). *Personal being*. Oxford, UK: Macmillan.

Lewis, M. D., & Granic, I. (Eds.) (2000). *Emotion, development, and self-organization: Dynamic systems approaches to emotional development*. Cambridge, UK: Cambridge University Press.

Mascolo, M. F. (2004a). *Synthesizing constructivist and sociocultural models of development: Analyzing the dynamic structure of joint acting, thinking and feeling*. Manuscript submitted for publication.

Mascolo, M. F. (2004b). The intersystemic construction of selves in cultures. In M. F. Mascolo & J. Li (Eds.), *Self and culture: Beyond dichotomization. New directions in child and adolescent development*. San Francisco, CA: Jossey-Bass.

Mascolo, M. F., & Fischer, K. W. (1998). The development of self through the co-ordination of component systems. In M. Ferrari & R. Sternberg (Eds.), *Self-awareness: Its nature and development* (pp. 332–384). New York: Guilford.

Mascolo, M. F., & Fischer, K. W. (in press). The new constructivism in cognitive development. To appear in B. Hopkins, R. G. Barre, G. F. Michel, & P. Rochat (Eds.), *Cambridge encyclopaedia of child development*. Cambridge, UK: Cambridge University Press.

Mascolo, M. F., Fischer, K. W., & Neimeyer, G. (1999). The dynamic co-development of intentionality, self and social relations. In J. Brandstadter & R. M. Lerner (Eds.), *Action and development: Origins and functions of intentional self-development* (pp. 133–166). Thousand Oaks, CA: Sage.

Mascolo, M. F., Fischer, K. W., & Li, J. (2003). The dynamic construction of emotion in development: A component systems approach. In R. J. Davidson, K. Scherer, & H. H. Goldsmith (Eds.), *Handbook of affective science*. Oxford, UK: Oxford University Press.

Moshman, D. (1998). Identity as a theory of oneself. *The Genetic Epistemologist, 26*(3), 1–10.

Newcomb, A. F., Bukowski, W. M., & Pattee, L. (1993). Children's peer relations: A meta-analytic review of popular, rejected, neglected, controversial, and average sociometric status. *Psychological Bulletin, 113*, 99–128.

Oyama, S. (2000). *Evolution's eye: A systems view on the biology–culture divide*. Durham, NC: Duke University Press.

Packer, M. J., & Scott, B. (1992). The hermeneutic investigation of peer relations. In T. Winegar & J. Valsinar (Eds.), *Children's development within social context: Vol. 2. Research and methodology*. Hillsdale, NJ: Lawrence Erlbaum Associates, Inc.

Pepler, D. J., & Craig, W. M. (1999). Understanding bullying and victimization from a dynamic systems perspective. In A. Slater & D. Muir (Eds.), *Developmental psychology: An advanced reader* (pp. 441–451). Oxford, UK: Blackwell.

Rogoff, B. (2003). *The cultural nature of human development.* Oxford, UK: Oxford University Press.

Rubin, K. H., Bukowski, W., & Parker, J. G. (1998). Peer interactions, relationships, and groups. In W. Damon (Series Ed.) & R. M. Lerner (Vol. Ed.), *Handbook of child psychology: Vol. 1. Theoretical models of human development* (5th ed., pp. 619–700). New York: Wiley.

Rubin, K. H., & Rose-Krasnor, L. (1992). Interpersonal problem solving and social competence in children. In V. B. Van Hasselt & M. Hersen (Eds.), *Handbook of social development.* New York: Plenum Press.

Sroufe, L. A., & Fleeson, J. (1986). Attachment and the construction of relationships. In W. Hartup & Z. Rubin (Eds.), *Relationships and development* (pp. 27–47). Hillsdale, NJ: Lawrence Erlbaum Associates, Inc.

Vygotsky, L. (1978). *Mind in society.* Cambridge, MA: Harvard University Press.

Wertsch, J. V (1998). *Mind as action.* Cambridge, UK: Cambridge University Press.

EUROPEAN JOURNAL OF DEVELOPMENTAL PSYCHOLOGY, 2004, *1*(4), 303–315

# Identity processing style, self-construction, and personal epistemic assumptions: A social-cognitive perspective

Michael D. Berzonsky

*Department of Psychology, State University of New York at Cortland, USA*

A social-cognitive model of identity is presented. Identity is conceptualized as a self-theory, a conceptual structure composed of self-representational and self-regulatory constructs. It is postulated that individuals have different identity processing styles and function as different types of self-theorists: information-oriented problem solvers and decision makers; normative types who conform to the prescriptions of significant others; and diffuse-avoidant theorists who procrastinate and attempt to avoid dealing with identity-relevant conflicts. The role that personal epistemic assumptions play in self-theorizing and the possibility that epistemic assumptions contribute to individual differences in identity style are considered.

> But what then am I? A thing which thinks. What is a thing that thinks? It is a thing which doubts, understands, affirms, [and] denies.
>
> Descartes (1642/1956)

René Descartes' (1596–1650) rational quest for certainty enabled him to affirm his own existence and it paved the way for contemporary cognitive conceptions of the self. For Descartes, thinking and doubting implied a self/mind that knows it thinks and doubts. The question of personal identity, however, involves more than consciousness; it implies a continuity of self-consciousness over time. Erik Erikson's (1968) notion of ego identity or William James' (1890/1950) self-as-knower represent the sense of identity that I wish to consider: The volitional and agentic *I* that thinks, wills, tests reality, and self-regulates.

Over the past four decades most identity research has been conducted within the identity status model developed by James Marcia (1966). Although Marcia defined identity in terms of the processes of self-

---

Correspondence should be addressed to Michael D. Berzonsky, Department of Psychology, State University of New York at Cortland, Cortland, New York 13045, USA.
E-mail: berzonskym@cortland.edu

http://www.tandf.co.uk/journals/pp/17405629.html          DOI: 10.1080/17405620444000120

exploration and commitment, most research has focused on the statuses as personality types or differential outcomes. In this paper a social-cognitive process model of identity is presented. Instead of focusing on characteristics of individuals with different identity statuses, the model highlights the role that social-cognitive strategies and processes play as individuals engage in or manage to avoid the process of constructing and revising a sense of identity. According to this view, identity is conceptualized as a structure as well as a process. Identity as a cognitive structure serves as a personal frame of reference for interpreting experience and self-relevant information and answering questions about the meaning, significance, and purpose of life. As a process, identity directs and governs the resources adolescents use to cope and adapt in everyday life (Berzonsky, 1990). When adaptive efforts fall short, negative feedback may create a need to revise or modify aspects of the identity structure. Accordingly, identity development is considered to involve an ongoing dialectical interchange between assimilative processes governed by the identity structure and accommodative processes directed by the social and physical contexts within which adolescents live and develop (Berzonsky, 1990, 1993). The model also postulates differences in how adolescents deal with or manage to avoid the tasks of maintaining and revising their sense of identity (Berzonsky, 1988, 1993). They rely on different social-cognitive processing orientations, or what I have termed identity styles (Berzonsky, 1989a, 1990). These processing styles reflect strategic differences in how individuals make decisions, deal with personal problems, and govern and regulate their lives.

## A SOCIAL-COGNITIVE MODEL OF IDENTITY

Following George Kelly (1955), Seymour Epstein (1980), and others, I have conceptualized identity as a self-theory, a self-constructed theory of oneself (Berzonsky, 1988, 1990). A self-theory is a conceptual structure made up of assumptions, postulates, and constructs relevant to the self interacting in the world (Epstein, 1980). It contains procedural knowledge or operative schemes for solving problems and making decisions, and representational schemas or personal constructs for understanding and making sense of events and personal experiences. Like formal theories, self-theories serve as the frame of reference for processing and interpreting the flux of self-relevant information encountered in the course of everyday life (Berzonsky, 1988, 1993).

### A constructivist view of identity

The model is based on the *constructivist* assumption that people actively play a role in constructing both who they *think* they are and the *reality* within which they live (Berzonsky, 1993). As Kelly (1955) noted, to understand experiences, people form personal constructs that govern the selection, organization, and understanding of environmental stimuli. Facts are not inherently meaningful, they are always interpreted within a system of constructs. Personal interpretations of events, not events-in-themselves constitute a person's reality. This does not imply that people can arbitrarily *make up* any identity that strikes their fancy. The model is grounded in a critical version of constructivism that assumes the existence of an empirical *reality* separate from the people who live and *interact* within it (Berzonsky, 1993). Reality, however, cannot be directly perceived or understood. A person's cognitive structures influence what information is attended to, encoded, and interpreted. External reality, however, constrains the viability or effectiveness of the constructs or theories that are generated: self and reality are co-constructed (Berzonsky, 1993; Kelly, 1955).

This view does not imply that adolescents or adults always theorize about themselves in a conscious or intentional fashion. Aspects of self-theories may be implicit and vaguely understood by their possessors. Nor does the model postulate that people can rationally construct a representation of their "true" or essential nature. Like formal theories, the validity of self-theories and theoretical constructs are evaluated in terms of functional utility: Do they provide explanations and interpretations that are personally believable and beneficial? Do they solve the problems and answer the questions they were constructed to deal with? Such functions include encoding self-relevant information and maintaining a coherent sense of self and reality; coping adaptively with personal stressors and conflicts; maintaining positive social relations with others; and effectively governing and regulating one's life (see Berzonsky, 1990; Epstein, 1980). Self-theories that effectively perform these functions, within particular physical and social contexts, are considered to be credible. Ineffective personal constructs will produce dissonant feedback signaling a need to revise aspects of the self-theory. A self-regulatory process is involved (Berzonsky, 1988, 1990).

## Identity processing orientations

The model highlights differences in how adolescents process self-relevant information, make decisions, solve problems, and construct and reconstruct their self-theories. Three social-cognitive processing orientations or identity styles have been identified: informational; normative; and diffuse-avoidant. Adolescents who utilize these orientations function as different types of self-theorists (see Berzonsky, 1989b, 1993).

Adolescents who use an *informational processing orientation* are self-reflective and they actively seek out and evaluate self-relevant information. They are information-oriented, self-explorers who want to learn things about themselves. They are skeptical about their self-constructions, open to new information, and willing to examine and revise aspects of their identity when faced with dissonant feedback (Berzonsky, 1989a, 1990). This mentally effortful approach to self-construction should lead to a self-theory comprised of relatively well differentiated and integrated constructs and postulates (Berzonsky, 1989b).

Not all adolescents handle decisions and self-diagnostic information in an open, effortful manner. Adolescents with a *normative processing orientation* conform to expectations, values, and prescriptions appropriated from significant others. Their primary goal is to protect existing self-views and to defend against information that may threaten *hard core* values and beliefs; they have a low tolerance for ambiguity and a high need to maintain structure and cognitive closure. This relatively automatic, or intuitive approach to self-construction should lead to a rigidly organized and crystallized self-theory composed of change-resistant, self-constructs (Berzonsky, 1989b).

A *diffuse-avoidant processing orientation* is characterized by procrastination and defensive avoidance: a reluctance to confront and face up to decisional situations, personal problems, and identity conflicts. Problems and decisions cannot always be avoided indefinitely. If adolescents delay long enough, behaviour will be influenced by social and physical demands and consequences. Such context-specific adjustments, however, are likely to involve short-term, ephemeral acts of behavioural conformity or verbal compliance rather than stable, long-term revisions in the identity structure. This processing style leads to a fragmented, inconsistent, or *empty* self-theory that constantly needs to be replenished by pleasurable experiences, consumer goods, approval from others, and the like (Berzonsky, 1994a).

## RESEARCH ON IDENTITY PROCESSING ORIENTATIONS

These identity processing orientations are postulated to operate on at least three levels (Berzonsky, 1990). The most basic level comprises the specific cognitive and behavioural responses individuals engage in when dealing with identity-relevant issues and conflicts. The middle level consists of social-cognitive strategies, which are integrated collections or systems of the more elemental behavioural and cognitive components. Identity style, the most general level, refers to the social-cognitive strategy that individuals characteristically use or would prefer to utilize (Berzonsky, 1990).

Most research has focused on the style level of the processing orientations. Identity styles are operationally defined by a self-report Identity Style Inventory (ISI; Berzonsky, 1989a, 1992). The ISI has been found to have adequate psychometric properties (see Berzonsky, 1992, 2003) and it, or translated versions of it, has been used in a variety of cultural contexts including the United States, the Czech Republic, Finland, Hungary, the Netherlands, Greece, India, Canada, Belgium, Spain, Turkey, and Australia (see Berzonsky, in press). It should be emphasized that no single measure can fully assess the range of theoretical complexity reflected in these identity processing orientations. The Identity Style Inventory (ISI) provides one way of marking some of the theoretical components that compose the general orientations. Some representative strands of research on identity styles will be briefly reviewed.

## Identity style and identity status

Most investigations of adolescent identity formation have been based on Marcia's (1966) four status types: achieved; diffusion; foreclosure; and moratorium. Relationships between identity style and identity status are perhaps the most consistently replicated findings in the identity-status literature. Self-exploring adolescents with an achievement or moratorium status have been found to have an informational style; foreclosures who have formed commitments without personal exploration, rely on a normative style; and non-exploring diffusions, who lack firm commitments, have been found to use a diffuse-avoidant style (Berzonsky, 1989a, 1990; Berzonsky & Adams, 1999; Berzonsky & Kuk, 2000; Berzonsky & Neimeyer, 1994; Schwartz, Mullis, Waterman, & Dunham, 2000; Streitmatter 1993). Informational scores also correlate positively with measures of identity-relevant processes like self-reflection, self-exploration, and introspection (Berzonsky, 1989a, 1990; Berzonsky & Sullivan, 1992).

## Self-definitional bases

Identity styles are also associated with the types of self-components youth use to define their sense of self (Berzonsky, 1994b; Berzonsky, Macek, & Nurmi, 2002). Specifically, informational youth emphasize personal self-attributes, e.g., *my values, my goals*, and *my standards*. Normative youth stress collective self-components, e.g., *my family, my religion*, and *my nationality*. Diffuse avoiders have been found to emphasize social self-elements, such as *my reputation* and *the impressions I make on others* (Berzonsky, 1994b; Berzonsky et al., 2002).

## Coping and decisional strategies

When confronted by stressful problems and conflicts, youth with an informational style rely on problem-focused strategies. They actively try to alter the stressful event or situation by, for instance, seeking relevant options, generating alternative solutions, attempting to resolve the problem, or by cognitively reinterpreting the situation (Berzonsky, 1990, 1992). In contrast, diffuse-avoiders use more reactive, emotion-focused tactics like denial, wishful thinking, or tension reduction (Berzonsky, 1992; Soenens, Duriez, & Goossens, 2003). Emotion-focused maneuvers are aimed at reducing emotional distress rather than solving or eliminating the stressor. In stressful situations, normative adolescents have been found to seek social support and reassurance (Berzonsky, 1992).

Decisional strategies used by youth with different identity styles have been found to parallel their coping efforts. An informational style is associated with effortful, vigilant decisions; diffuse-avoidance is related to pre-decisional anxiety, procrastination, and avoidance (Berzonsky & Ferrari, 1996). Diffuse-avoiders are reluctant to assume personal responsibility for decisions that go awry; they rationalize and make excuses for poor decisions and they engage in self-handicapping behaviours (Berzonsky, 1994c; Berzonsky & Ferrari, 1996).

## Identity styles and cognitive strategies

A number of studies have investigated cognitive correlates of identity style. Diffuse-avoidance is associated with maladaptive cognitive and attributional strategies like external control expectancies, low self-efficacy, self-handicapping, task avoidance, and a tendency to engage in task-irrelevant behaviours (Berzonsky, 1990, 1994c; Berzonsky, Nurmi, Tammi, & Kinney, 1999; Nurmi, Berzonsky, Tammi, & Kinney, 1997). Although both informational and normative youth have been found to be conscientious, goal directed, and reasonably adaptive in their lives, they have been found to differ in openness to new experiences, need for cognition, need for structure, and the extent to which they rely on rational/analytical processes (Berzonsky, 1990; Berzonsky & Ferrari, 1996; Berzonsky & Kinney, 1995; Berzonsky & Sullivan, 1992; Dollinger, 1995).

These findings are consistent with the view that style assessments measure different identity processes and reflect different social-cognitive strategies. Relationships between identity processing styles and implicit epistemological assumptions will now be considered.

## IDENTITY STYLE AND PERSONAL EPISTEMIC ASSUMPTIONS

Modern philosophers of science have underscored the constructive nature of scientific theory testing. Imre Lakatos (1972), for instance, maintains that a *hard core* of non-falsifiable values and assumptions dictates what constitutes a problem, how it can legitimately be investigated, and what standards will determine whether solutions are effective. Likewise, youth with different identity processing styles have been found to hold different implicit assumptions about themselves, knowledge, and the world (Berzonsky, 1993, 1994a).

Information-oriented youth have been found to endorse constructivist epistemological assumptions and to hold an organic world view (Berzonsky, 1993, Berzonsky, 1994a; Caputi & Oades, 2001). They assume they play an active role in constructing who they are: they define themselves in terms of their own values, goals, self-knowledge, and unique psychological states (Berzonsky, 1994b; Berzonsky et al., 2002).

Normative youth hold a mechanistic view of the world; reality is seen as objective, reliable, and deterministic (Berzonsky, 1993, 1994a; Caputi & Oades, 2001). They view themselves as passive agents whose personalities are determined by social forces. They hold clear-cut, absolute views about truth and self and they define themselves in terms of collective self-attributes like religion, family, and country (Berzonsky, 1994b; Berzonsky et al., 2002).

The epistemic stance of diffuse-avoidant self-theorists is less clear. In one investigation, diffuse-avoiders endorsed a formistic world view, suggesting they view who they are as being predetermined by fate or factors beyond their control (Berzonsky, 1994a, Study 3). Other findings indicate that they view knowledge and the world as a chaotic, multiplicity of options that provide a limited basis for legitimate certainty or rational judgments (Berzonsky, 1994c). Given this multiplicity of options, diffuse-avoiders rely primarily on personal preferences, hedonistic desires, and emotional feelings: They define themselves in terms of social self-attributes like reputation, popularity, and the impressions they make on others (Berzonsky, 1994b; Berzonsky et al., 2002).

## THE DEVELOPMENT OF A CONSTRUCTIVIST VIEW OF KNOWING

Since personal epistemic assumptions play a role in the identity style adolescents employ, research on the development of epistemic assumptions may be relevant to developmental questions about identity styles. Different researchers have concluded that, developmentally, a realistic epistemic view of absolute *Truth* gives way to a subjective, interpretative view of relativistic *truth*. There is controversy, however, about when constructivist epistemic beliefs first emerge.

### Do preschool children hold a constructive theory of mind?

Research with false-belief tasks indicates that 4- to 5-year-old children realize others can hold beliefs different from their own and that personal beliefs, even false ones, influence how people act (Flavell & Miller, 1998). Based on findings like these, some investigators have concluded that preschool children assume that thoughts and beliefs are actively constructed in someone's mind (Wellman & Hickling, 1994). However, realizing that people exposed to different information—which typically occurs in a false-belief task—hold different beliefs does not necessarily require a constructivist theory of mind: a mechanical *copy theory* of mind can lead to the same conclusion (Carpendale & Chandler, 1996). Understanding that people exposed to the same information may construct different but equally credible interpretations appears to occur during adolescence.

## Epistemic development in adolescence

Several investigators have postulated that epistemic development proceeds through three *general* levels in which first realistic (absolute) criteria, then subjective criteria, and finally a combination of realistic and subjective considerations are highlighted (Hofer & Pintrich, 1997). This third level, where objective evidence and rational arguments can be used to justify subjective beliefs, is consistent with the information-oriented view of constructivism that I have advanced. The first two levels, at least on a global scale, correspond to the realistic, authority-based view of knowledge associated with a normative identity style, and the subjective but arbitrary stance adopted by diffuse-avoiders (Berzonsky, 1993, 1994a).

Although there are age differences in epistemic stances, differences within age groups have been found starting in early adolescence (Hofer & Pintrich, 1997; Kitchener & King, 2002; Kuhn, Cheney, & Weinstock, 2000). For example, in a study of 10- to 40-year-old participants, Kuhn et al. (2000) found that at least some 10-year-old children adopted a constructivist epistemic posture, and at least some 20- to 40-year-old adults adopted an absolutist stance.

The research of Michael Chandler and his colleagues is relevant to the present discussion because it links rational thinking, epistemic development and identity formation. Chandler, Boyes, and Ball (1990, Study 1) found a strong relationship between Piagetian formal-operational reasoning and epistemic level among teenage adolescents. All of the concrete-operational adolescents held realistic epistemological assumptions, only 10% of the formal reasoners did (see also Boyes & Chandler, 1992). Chandler et al. (1990, Study 2) also found a relationship between epistemic beliefs and identity classifications. Seventy-five percent of the realists were classified as either identity foreclosures or diffusions; 76% of the adolescents who scored above the realism level were categorized as self-exploring identity achievers or moratoriums (see also Boyes & Chandler, 1992).

Given the reliable relationship between identity status and identity style, these findings suggest that the pattern of relationships found between epistemological assumptions and identity style with late adolescents (Berzonsky, 1993, 1994a), may already be present in early adolescence. Pre-adolescents who generally hold realistic epistemic assumptions, also adopt a foreclosed, normative identity style; they rely on authorities to determine Truth. During adolescence, changes in the rational/analytical processing system, as measured by formal-operational tasks, enhance decisional and problem-solving effectiveness, and undermine the foundational underpinnings of realistic epistemic assumptions (Boyes & Chandler, 1992; Chandler et al., 1990). These changes in rational/analytical thinking are *not* necessarily due to the emergence of a structured ensemble of logical operations as postulated by Inhelder and Piaget (1958). Developmental changes in rational/analytical thinking may be due to a number of factors including changes in information-processing capacity or functional efficiency, increased organization and consolidation of conceptual knowledge, acquisition of domain-specific expertise, mastery of new symbolic representational systems, and so on (see Case, 1998). Chandler also cautioned against too literal an interpretation of the term formal operations (Chandler, Hallett, & Sokol, 2002).

Research indicates that virtually all *normal* late adolescents may possess the meta-representational competence and rational thinking strategies that constitute an informational identity processing orientation (Berzonsky, 1998; Berzonsky & Ferrari, 1996). The development of these cognitive resources during adolescence, as operationalized by performance on formal-reasoning tasks, is also associated with a shift to a more subjective and, perhaps, a more constructivist and relativistic epistemic stance (Chandler et al., 1990). Of course, it is one thing for adolescents to assume that the validity of conflicting claims about the same movie depends on the tastes and preferences of the viewers. Those same adolescents may not necessarily assume that the credibility of competing claims about how much an object weighs, when an event happened, or whether two plus three equals five (2 + 3 = 5), depends, respectively, on the gravitational field, spatial location, and number system relevant to those claims. There is a need to investigate the process by which domain-specific relativistic assumptions are transformed into more generic relativistic assumptions about the process of knowing across domains (see also Chandler et al., 1990).

## CONCLUDING REMARKS

According to the social-cognitive model presented in the present paper, individuals differ in how they approach or avoid the tasks of constructing and reconstructing a sense of identity and those differences are hypothesized to play a role in how effectively they deal with various identity functions like coping with personal problems, resolving conflicts and stressors, maintaining a coherent sense of self, establishing social relations, and successfully governing and regulating their lives. Taken together, the data reviewed in the present paper are consistent with that view.

Youth with an informational identity style have consistently been found to have a relatively high need for cognition, to rely on rational/analytic processing when making decisions and dealing with identity-relevant issues, and to have an achieved identity status (Berzonsky, 1990; Berzonsky & Neimeyer, 1994; Berzonsky & Sullivan, 1992). In contrast, normative youth have a high need for structure and a low tolerance for ambiguity; they tend to be relatively closed-minded, foreclosed individuals who are motivated to process self-relevant information in biased fashion designed to preserve existing self-constructs (Berzonsky & Kinney, 1995; Berzonsky & Sullivan, 1992; Soenens et al., 2003). Not only do diffuse-avoidant youth lack a well organized and coherent system of beliefs or convictions, they strategically attempt to avoid negative self-relevant feedback. They tend to react in an impulsive or indifferent fashion and are quick to make excuses and deny responsibility for negative outcomes (Berzonsky, 1994c). As might be expected, youth who rely on a diffuse-avoidant identity style appear to be at increased risk for a host of behavioural and personal problems including poor peer relations, academic difficulties, low self-esteem, drug and alcohol problems, depressive reactions, neuroticism, disordered eating, and conduct disorders (Adams et al., 2002; Berzonsky & Kuk, 2000; Dollinger, 1995; Jones, Ross, & Hartmann, 1992; Nurmi et al., 1997; Wheeler, Adams, & Keating, 2001; White & Jones, 1996).

Generally, use of both informational and normative styles is positively associated with firm goals, commitments, a sense of direction and purpose, and relatively effective behaviour (Adams et al., 2002; Berzonsky, 1998, 2003; Berzonsky & Kuk, 2000; Dollinger, 1995). However, the more adolescents are expected to assume personal responsibility for setting their own priorities and monitoring their own behaviour, especially in diverse and changing environmental contexts, the less adaptive a normative orientation may become (Berzonsky & Kuk, 2000). Information-oriented youth may also be better at establishing mature interpersonal relationships; they display more tolerance of others and less need for continual approval and reassurance than normative youth (Berzonsky, 1998; Berzonsky & Kuk, 2000).

The available data also indicate that youth with different identity styles hold different implicit epistemological assumptions about themselves and the world within which they live and develop. If, as Chandler et al. (1990) postulate, the development of higher-order analytical reasoning during adolescence normally undermines absolutist, realistic epistemic assumptions, it raises the question about why some adolescents respond by adopting a subjective, but intellectually arbitrary, stance (diffuse-avoidant style), whereas others resort to more dogmatic or automatic conformity (normative style), and yet others take a rational constructivist position (informational style)? Although definitive answers are not available, some areas for future research include motivational variables, family influences (Berzonsky, 2004), educational contextual demands (King & Kitchener, 2002), and genetic-based dispositions (see, e.g., Jang, Livesley, & Vernon, 1996).

In conclusion, there is a need to longitudinally investigate developmental changes in both the social-cognitive strategies that adolescents use when processing self-relevant information and the strategies that they prefer to use (i.e., their identity style). What is the normal course of development of identity processing orientations during adolescence and adulthood? How stable are processing orientations across the life span? What factors contribute to interindividual differences in processing orientation?

## REFERENCES

Adams, G. R., Munro, B., Doherty-Poirer, M., Munro, G., Petersen, A.-M. R., & Edwards, J. (2001). Diffuse/avoidance, normative, and informational identity styles: Using identity theory to predict maladjustment. *Identity*, *1*, 307–320.

Berzonsky, M. D. (1988). Self-theorists, identity status, and social cognition. In D. K. Lapsley & F. C. Power (Eds.), *Self, ego, and identity: Integrative approaches* (pp. 243–262). New York: Springer-Verlag.

Berzonsky, M. D. (1989a). Identity style: Conceptualization and measurement. *Journal of Adolescent Research*, *4*, 267–281.

Berzonsky, M. D. (1989b). The self as a theorist: Individual differences in identity formation. *International Journal of Personal Construct Psychology*, *2*, 363–376.

Berzonsky, M. D. (1990). Self-construction over the life-span: A process perspective on identity formation. In G. J. Neimeyer & R. A. Neimeyer (Eds.), *Advances in personal construct psychology* (Vol. 1, pp. 155–186). Greenwich, CT: JAI.

Berzonsky, M. D. (1992). Identity style and coping strategies. *Journal of Personality*, *60*, 771–788.

Berzonsky, M. D. (1993). A constructivist view of identity development: People as post-positivist self-theorists. In J. Kroger (Ed.), *Discussions on ego identity* (pp. 169–183). Hillsdale, NJ: Lawrence Erlbaum Associates, Inc.

Berzonsky, M. D. (1994a). Individual differences in self-construction: The role of constructivist epistemological assumptions. *Journal of Constructivist Psychology*, *7*, 263–281.

Berzonsky, M. D. (1994b). Self-identity: The relationship between process and content. *Journal of Research in Personality*, *28*, 453–460.

Berzonsky, M. D. (1994c, July). *A diffuse/avoidant identity processing style: Confused self or self-serving strategy?* Paper presented at the Biennial Meetings of the International Society for the Study of Behavioural Development, Amsterdam, The Netherlands.

Berzonsky, M. D. (1998, July). *Psychosocial development in early adulthood: The transition to university.* Paper presented at the Biennial Meetings of the International Society for the Study of Behavioural Development, Berne, Switzerland.

Berzonsky, M. D. (2003). Identity style and well-being: Does commitment matter? *Identity: An International Journal of Theory and Research, 3*, 131–142.

Berzonsky, M. D. (2004). Identity style, parental authority, and identity commitment. *Journal of Youth and Adolescence, 33*, 213–220.

Berzonsky, M. D. (in press). Identity processing style and self-definition: Effects of a priming manipulation. *Polish Psychology Bulletin.*

Berzonsky, M. D., & Adams, G. R. (1999). The identity status paradigm: Still useful after thirty-five years. *Developmental Review, 19*, 557–590.

Berzonsky, M. D., & Ferrari, J. R. (1996). Identity orientation and decisional strategies. *Personality and Individual Differences, 20*, 597–606.

Berzonsky, M. D., & Kinney, A. (1995, February). *Identity style and need for cognitive closure.* Paper presented at the Biennial Meetings of the Society for Research on Identity Formation, Dog Island, FL.

Berzonsky, M. D., & Kuk, L. S. (2000). Identity status, identity processing style, and the transition to university. *Journal of Adolescent Research, 15*, 81–98.

Berzonsky, M. D., Macek, P., & Nurmi, J.-E. (2003). Interrelations among identity process, content, and structure: A cross-cultural investigation. *Journal of Adolescent Research, 18*, 112–130.

Berzonsky, M. D., & Neimeyer, G. J. (1994). Ego identity status and identity processing orientation: The moderating role of commitment. *Journal of Research in Personality, 28*, 425–435.

Berzonsky, M. D., Nurmi, J.-E., Kinney, A., & Tammi, K. (1999). Identity processing orientation and cognitive and behavioral strategies: Similarities and differences across different contexts. *European Journal of Personality, 13*, 105–120.

Berzonsky, M. D., & Sullivan, C. (1992). Social-cognitive aspects of identity style: Need for cognition, experiential openness, and introspection. *Journal of Adolescent Research, 7*, 140–155.

Boyes, M. C., & Chandler, M. J. (1992). Cognitive development, epistemic doubt, and identity formation in adolescence. *Journal of Youth and Adolescence, 21*, 277–304.

Caputi, P., & Oades, L. (2001). Epistemic assumptions: Understanding the self in the world (a note on the relationship between identity style, world view, and constructivist assumptions using an Australian sample). *Journal of Constructivist Psychology, 14*, 127–134.

Carpendale, J. I., & Chandler, M. J. (1996). On the distinction between false belief understanding and subscribing to an interpretive theory of mind. *Child Development, 67*, 1686–1706.

Case, R. (1998). The development of conceptual structures. In D. Kuhn & R. S. Siegler (Vol. Eds.), W. Damon (Series Ed.), *Handbook of child psychology: Vol. 2. Cognition, perception, and language* (5th ed., pp. 745–800). New York: Wiley.

Chandler, M. J., Boyes, M., & Ball, L. (1990). Relativism and stations of epistemic doubt. *Journal of Experimental Child Psychology, 50*, 370–395.

Descartes, R. (1642/1956). *Meditations on first philosophy.* Excerpted in M. Rader (Ed.), *The enduring questions* (pp. 53–75). New York: Holt, Rinehart, and Winston.

Dollinger, S. M. (1995). Identity styles and the five-factor model of personality. *Journal of Research in Personality, 29*, 475–479.

Epstein, S. (1980). The self-concept: A review and the proposal of and integrated theory of personality. In E. Staub (Ed.), *Personality: Basic aspects and current research* (pp. 81–132). Englewood Cliffs, NJ: Prentice-Hall.

Erikson, E. (1968). *Identity: Youth and crisis.* New York: Norton.

Flavell, J. H., & Miller, P. H. (1998). Social cognition. In D. Kuhn & R. S. Siegler (Vol. Eds.), W. Damon (Series Ed.), *Handbook of child psychology: Vol. 2. Cognition, perception, and language* (5th ed., pp. 851–898). New York: Wiley.

Hofer, B. K., & Pintrich, P. R. (1997). The development of epistemological theories: Beliefs about knowledge and knowing and their relation to learning. *Review of Educational Research, 67*, 88–140.

Inhelder, B., & Piaget, J. (1958). *The growth of logical thinking from childhood to adolescence.* New York: Basic Books.

James, W. (1890/1950). *The principles of psychology.* New York: Dover.

Jang, K. L., Livesley, W. J., & Vernon, P. A. (1996). Heritability of the big five personality dimensions and their facets: A twin study. *Journal of Personality, 64*, 577–591.

Jones, R. M., Ross, C. N., & Hartmann, B. R. (1992). An investigation of cognitive style and alcohol/work-related problems among naval personnel. *Journal of Drug Education, 22*, 241–251.

Kelly, G. A. (1955). *The psychology of personal constructs.* New York: Norton.

King, P. M., & Kitchener, K. S. (2002). The reflective judgment model: Twenty years of research on epistemic cognition. In B. K. Hofer & P. R. Pintrich (Eds.), *Personal epistemology: The psychology of beliefs about knowledge and knowing* (pp. 37–61). Mahwah, NJ: Lawrence Erlbaum Associates, Inc.

Kuhn, D., Cheney, R., & Weinstock, M. (2000). The development of epistemological understanding. *Cognitive Development, 15*, 309–328.

Lakatos, I. (1970). Falsification and the methodology of scientific research programmes. In I. Lakatos & A. Musgrave (Eds.), *Criticism and the growth of knowledge* (pp. 91–196). Cambridge: Cambridge University Press.

Marcia, J. E. (1966). Development and validation of ego identity status. *Journal of Personality and Social Psychology, 3*, 551–558.

Nurmi, J.-E., Berzonsky, M. D., Tammi, K., & Kinney, A. (1997). Identity processing orientation, cognitive and behavioral strategies and well-being. *International Journal of Behavioral Development, 21*, 555–570.

Schwartz, S. J., Mullis, R. L., Waterman, A. S., & Dunham, R. M. (2000). Ego identity status, identity style, and personal expressiveness: An empirical investigation of three convergent constructs. *Journal of Adolescent Research, 15*, 504–521.

Soenens, B., Duriez, B., & Goossens, L. (2003). *Social-psychological profiles of identity styles: Attitudinal and social-cognitive correlates in late adolescence.* Manuscript submitted for publication.

Streitmatter, J. (1993). Identity status and identity style: A replication study. *Journal of Adolescence, 16*, 211–215.

Wheeler, H. A., Adams, G. R., & Keating, L. (2001). Binge eating as a means for evading identity issues: The association between an avoidance identity style and bulimic behavior. *Identity, 1*, 161–178.

Wellman, H. M., & Hickling, A. K. (1994). The mind's 'I': Children's conceptions of the mind as an active agent. *Child Development, 65*, 1564–1580.

White, J. M., & Jones, R. M. (1996). Identity styles of male inmates. *Criminal Justice and Behavior, 23*, 490–504.

EUROPEAN JOURNAL OF DEVELOPMENTAL PSYCHOLOGY, 2004, *1*(4), 317–330

# Adolescents' conceptions of family democracy: Does their own behaviour play a role?

Stefan Persson, Håkan Stattin, and Margaret Kerr

*Örebro University, Sweden*

Much research on family democracy has started from the assumption that parents produce the democratic climate and adolescent behaviour is an outcome of it. In this study, we asked whether and how adolescent behaviour contributes to family democracy, using both parents' and adolescents' behaviours as predictors of family democracy. Participants were 1057 fifteen to sixteen year olds and their parents. Results showed that adolescents' conceptions of family democracy involve both their own and their parents' behaviour. When controlling for parents' behaviours, adolescents' behaviours added significantly to the prediction of democracy. Parents' warmth and the adolescents' openness to communication seem to be two major aspects of the democratic workings in the family. Hence, the democratic workings of the family cannot be described fully if adolescents' behaviour is ignored.

Few would argue with the assertion that parents set up the rearing conditions in the family that help shape their children's behaviour. Parents' own family histories, their philosophies of childrearing, and other factors probably determine what sorts of family climates they create. One might ask, however, whether children or adolescents themselves contribute in setting up the family climate. There is much evidence that parents respond to the characteristics of their infants and young children and adjust their behaviour accordingly (e.g., Anderson, Lytton, & Romney, 1986; Bell & Chapman, 1986, for a review; Dix, Ruble, Grusec, & Nixon, 1986; McHale, Kavanaugh, & Berkman, 2003; Teti & Gelfland, 1991; van den Boom & Hoeksma, 1994). There is also evidence that, for parents of adolescents, specific parenting behaviours are partly reactions to adolescents' characteristics (e.g., Ge et al., 1996; Kerr & Stattin, 2003; Kim, Conger, Lorenz, & Elder, 2001; Neiderhiser, Reiss, Hetherington, & Plomin, 1999). Is it not

---

Address correspondence to Stefan Persson, Department of Behavioural, Social and Legal Sciences, Örebro University, Fakultetsgatan 1, SE 701 82 Örebro, Sweden. Email: stefan.persson@bsr.oru.se

http://www.tandf.co.uk/journals/pp/17405629.html    DOI: 10.1080/17405620444000238

reasonable, then, to think that the overall family climate is determined by the child's characteristics as well as by those of the parents? In this study, we focus on family democracy, an aspect of the family climate that consistently has been attributed to parents. We look at youths' judgments about whether their families are democratic, and we ask whether their own behaviour, in addition to their parents', is part of the conceptualization.

Democracy has long been considered important for child and adolescent development, but creating a democratic climate implicitly has been considered something that parents alone are responsible for. Baldwin's early work on democratic parenting, for example, made this assumption by using parental behaviours to define democratic homes. Children's behaviours were used as outcomes of democratic or undemocratic rearing, revealing the implicit assumption that parents alone create a democratic family climate (Baldwin, 1955). Later, parenting-styles researchers discussed democratic parenting as one critical aspect of authoritative parenting that explained its connection to children's good adjustment (e.g., Baumrind, 1968). But, again, in this work, the democratic climate was considered under parents' control, and the child's behaviour was considered an outcome of the experiences of negotiation that parents provided through their democratic parenting.

In modern parenting research, democracy appears often as an important part of the family climate, but it also seems to be fairly deeply entrenched in people's thinking as something that *parents* do or create. For example, democratic issues appear in family functioning scales (Bloom, 1985; Noller, Seth-Smith, Bouma, & Schweitzer, 1992) with items such as: "in our family, parents did not check with the children before making important decisions" and "children have a say in rules". In parenting-styles research, the term family democracy is used interchangeably with the term parental autonomy granting, thus revealing the assumption that family democracy is a quality of parents rather than the family (e.g., Gray & Steinberg, 1999, Steinberg, 2001; Steinberg, Mounts, Lamborn, & Dornbusch, 1991). Although this research does not explicitly state that parents alone create a democratic family climate, it does so implicitly by leaving child characteristics out of the measures and considering child adjustment as an outcome.

Another relevant line of research is on family decision making, and studies in this area have attended more to adolescents' active roles than the studies reviewed above. Some have theorized that it is important for parents to change over time in response to adolescents' increasing needs for input into decisions (Baumrind, 1991; Eccles et al., 1991; Holmbeck, Paikoff, & Brooks-Gunn, 1995; Steinberg, 1990) and some have looked at these changes empirically (e.g., Fuligni & Eccles, 1993; Eccles et al., 1991). The main research questions in these studies, however, have been about how the fit between adolescents' needs for input and the input parents allow relates to adjustment, and not whether adolescents' behaviours affect the amount of input they have. On the other hand, some studies have looked at how adolescents' characteristics affect the input they get into decisions, but the characteristics they have considered—gender, pubertal status, and birth order (Bumpus, Crouter, & McHale, 2001); adjustment to junior high school (Fuligni & Eccles, 1993); and problem behaviour (Lamborn, Dornbusch, & Steinberg, 1996)—do not directly tap adolescents' roles in creating a democratic climate. And again, the main research questions have been how family decision making affects youth adjustment. Thus, the idea that the degree of democracy in the family might be directly attributable to *both* parents and adolescents has not been tested.

There are several parents' and youths' behaviours that, theoretically, should strengthen or undermine the democratic workings of the family. In the literature on family democracy, much focus is on whether children have a say in decisions and can express and develop opinions (Bloom, 1985; Gray & Steinberg, 1999; Noller et al., 1992). If parents react negatively to the youth's communication and try to control the youth's behaviour by inducing guilt instead of discussing and making joint decisions, the youth should feel that it is not possible to express or develop opinions. On the other hand, both parents' expressions of emotional warmth and their willingness to talk about themselves should encourage youths to communicate openly and express their opinions. Finally, if parents are to involve their children in decisions and talk about themselves it is likely that they need to feel that they can trust their children. These specific parenting behaviours, then, might strengthen or undermine the interactions that have in the literature been considered central to family democracy.

Likewise, there are several youth characteristics that might strengthen or undermine the democratic workings of the family. Adolescents' openness to communication should be an important aspect of the democratic workings of the family. If adolescents are willing to talk about their lives and want their parents to be involved, parents should be likely to have good knowledge concerning the youths. Having good knowledge concerning the youth should make it easier for parents to be involved in making decisions together with the youth. Furthermore, parents' knowledge has been linked to the amount of trust that parents have in their adolescents (Kerr, Stattin, & Trost, 1999). However, if adolescents lie, try to manipulate others, or fail to accept responsibility for their own actions, parents would be unlikely to trust and respect the youth and the youth's word and the family would be less likely to be democratic. Additionally, if youths do not show acceptance or respect for family rules, parents could respond by behaving unilaterally, thus excluding youths when making decisions. Thus, these youth characteristics might also help to determine whether the family climate is democratic.

In this study, we ask whether parental characteristics are the sole determinants of adolescents' conceptions of family democracy. To the extent that they are, they should explain why some adolescents perceive their families to be democratic whereas others do not, and once parenting behaviours are taken into account, adolescent characteristics should not be important. However, to the extent that adolescents' behaviour helps to define the democratic family, both parent and adolescent characteristics should help differentiate adolescents who perceive their families to be democratic organizations from those who do not.

# METHOD

## Participants

A complete age cohort in a city in central Sweden participated in the present study. They were all 9th graders in the city schools (15–16 year olds). Youths took part in the study unless their parents returned a form stating that they did not want their youth to participate. The participation rate was 83% ($N = 1057$; 48% boys, 52% girls) for adolescents and 67% for their parents. Adolescents completed questionnaires during an average school day. Parents filled out questionnaires at home and returned them by mail.

## Measures

Many of these measures have been described in full elsewhere (Kerr & Stattin, 2003; Kerr et al., 1999; Stattin & Kerr, 2000). Others are reported for the first time in this study (family government style; parents' guilt induction; parental self-disclosure).

## Family government style

We asked youths about the government styles of their families: "If you see your family as a country, what type of government does your family have? Think of your family as a country and the parents as the leaders". The response options were: (1) "It is a democracy where people respect each other and people discuss and make decisions together. Sometimes conflicts can arise, but people try to solve them together. Everyone can influence decisions"; (2) "It is a dictatorship where there are leaders that decide over everyone. Only the leaders can influence the decisions"; (3) "It is an anarchy where everyone does what he or she wants to do. There are no clear rules and there is no leader"; and (4) "It is a country where people have had a revolution. The people who used to make decisions do not make the decisions now. The old leaders no longer have any power". The majority perceived their families as democracies (72%). Some saw their families as dictatorships (12%) or anarchies (12%), and 4% said that a revolution had taken place.

## Parental behaviour that could undermine or strengthen a democratic system

*Parents' negative reactions to information.*   Adolescents responded to items such as: "Have you ever told your parents things and later regretted it?" and "Have your parents ever used what you told them against you?" (alpha = .83).

*Parents' guilt induction.*   Here, we asked: "What happens if you do something that your parents really dislike?" Youths responded to a list of statements, eight of which indicated guilt induction (e.g., "They do not talk to me for awhile", "They are silent and cold toward me"). The alpha reliability was .90.

*Parental warmth.*   Adolescents responded to seven statements such as: "They praise me for no special reason" and "They show with words and gestures that they like me" (alpha = .83).

*Trust.*   Parents answered eight questions such as: "Do you trust that your child will not hang out with bad people?" and "Do you trust that your child will be careful with his/her money?" (alpha = .83).

*Parental self-disclosure.*   Parents answered eight questions about their self-disclosure to their children such as: "If you are worried about something having to do with the family, do you let your child know about it?" and "Do you often talk with your child about things that are personally important to you?" (alpha = .82).

## Adolescents' characteristics that could strengthen or undermine democracy

*Openness to communication.*   The adolescent's openness to communication was measured by aggregating two disclosure scales, one assessing disclosing feelings and thoughts and the other assessing disclosure of behaviours outside home. *Adolescent disclosure of feelings and thoughts* was measured with seven items, including: "Do you tell your mom or dad how you really feel inside?" and "If something bothers you, do you want your parents to know about it?" *Adolescent disclosure of information about daily activities* included items such as: "Do you talk at home about how you are doing in the different subjects in school?" and "Do you keep a lot of secrets from your parents about what you do during your free time?" The composite measure had an alpha reliability of .83.

*Adolescents' disclosure of information about daily activities* was also assessed by the parents. Parents answered the same five questions as their children, with only minor changes in wording where necessary; this measure will be referred to as "parent-reported openness to communication" (alpha = .78).

*Defiance.*   Parents responded to seven questions such as: "What does the child usually do when you as parents tell him/her to stop doing something that you don't like?" (responses ranged from "Stops immediately" to "Doesn't listen at all"); "What happens if you as parents tell the child that he/she isn't allowed to go out a particular night—but the child has already promised his/her friends to come out?" (responses ranged from "The child listens to you and stays home" to "The child doesn't listen to you and goes out anyway"). Alpha reliability was .76.

*Undesirable personality.*   We created a composite measure consisting of four personality characteristics: lying; callousness; irresponsibility; and failure to take responsibility for one's actions. The composite measure had an alpha reliability of .90. The individual scales are described below. *Lying, callousness*, and *irresponsibility* were 5-item subscales of the Youth Psychopathic Traits Inventory (Andershed, Kerr, Stattin, & Levander, 2002). They included items such as: "Sometimes I lie for no reason, other than because it's fun" and "I've often gotten into trouble because I've lied too much" (lying; alpha = .83); "I think that crying is a sign of weakness, even if no one sees you" and "When other people have problems, it is often their own fault, therefore one should not help them" (callousness; alpha = .72); and "I often don't or didn't have my school or work assignments done on time" and "I have often been late to work or classes in school" (irresponsibility; alpha = .66). *Failure to assume blame* for one's mistakes was measured with five items, including: "When I've done something that's hurt someone, they usually exaggerate and make it seem worse that it really was" and "I'm always getting blamed for things that aren't my fault" (alpha = .80).

## Psychometric properties of the measures

The measures used in this study have adequate reliabilities, as shown by the alphas reported above. Additionally, in a study in progress, for a representative sample of adolescents of the same age (Kerr, Stattin, & Kiesner, 2004) we have one-year stabilities of several of the measures used in this study ($n$ = 486). A cross-tabulation yielded a phi of .59 over one year for family government style. The one-year stabilities were .37 for guilt induction, .47 for parents' negative reactions to information, .58 for parental warmth, .64 for adolescent disclosure of feelings and thoughts, and .65 for adolescent disclosure of information about daily activities (all $ps$ < .001).

Concerning validity, our measures related to each other in predictable ways (see Table 1). In addition, when parents and youths both reported on adolescents' openness to communication, they agreed substantially, $r$ = .47, $p$ < .001.

# RESULTS

## Can parents' behaviours predict a democratic family climate?

To answer this question, we used a dichotomized measure of family government style in which democracy was contrasted with three undemocratic options. Using a logistic regression model, we predicted this measure from the five dimensions of parents' behaviour. As Table 2 shows, all parental behaviours except parental disclosure were significant predictors of family democracy from the youths' points of view. Parents' warmth was the strongest predictor and it increased the likelihood that the adolescent would view the family as democratic. Having parents who did not trust the adolescent, reacted negatively to information, or used guilt-inducing behaviours decreased the likelihood. With a .75 cut off, the model correctly predicted 70.2% of the youths who reported their families to be undemocratic and 72.2% of those who reported their families to be democratic. The total percentage of correct predictions was 71.7%, Nagelkerke $R^2$ = .26. Thus, these results suggest that parents' behaviours are, indeed, important in adolescents' conceptualizations of family democracy.

## Can youths' behaviours predict a democratic family climate?

We then took the opposite point of view and asked whether youths' characteristics predicted their judgments of family democracy. Again, we used the dichotomized measure of family government style as a dependent variable with the four youth behaviours—adolescent and parent reported openness to communication, defiance, and undesirable personality—as

## TABLE 1
### Intercorrelations among the measures used in the study

| | Parent behaviours | | | | | Adolescent behaviours | | |
| | Trust (P) | Negative reactions (Y) | Guilt induction (Y) | Warmth (Y) | Open to com. (Y) | Open to com. (P) | Defiance (P) | Undesirable personality (Y) |
|---|---|---|---|---|---|---|---|---|
| Parental disclosure (P) | .19 | −.04 | −.11 | .22 | .23 | .36 | −.30 | −.09 |
| Trust (P) | | −.20 | −.20 | .22 | .24 | .40 | −.39 | −.38 |
| Negative reactions (Y) | | | .48 | −.27 | −.31 | −.17 | .22 | .41 |
| Guilt induction (Y) | | | | −.40 | −.37 | −.19 | .24 | .42 |
| Warmth (Y) | | | | | .51 | .29 | −.27 | −.27 |
| Openness to com. (Y) | | | | | | .47 | −.32 | −.46 |
| Openness to com. (P) | | | | | | | −.62 | −.27 |
| Defiance (P) | | | | | | | | .27 |

(P) = parent-reported; (Y) = youth-reported. All correlations are significant at the .001 level, except the following correlations with parental disclosure: negative reactions (ns); guilt induction (p = .004); and undesirable personality (ns).

TABLE 2
Logistic regression model predicting democratic versus
undemocratic family climate from parents' behaviour

| Parent behaviour | Wald statistic | $p \leqslant$ |
|---|---|---|
| Parental disclosure (P) | 0.18 | ns |
| Trust (P) | 10.48 | .001 |
| Negative reactions (Y) | 7.68 | .006 |
| Guilt induction (Y) | 8.02 | .005 |
| Warmth (Y) | 57.05 | < .001 |

(P) = parent-reported; (Y) = youth-reported.

independent measures. As shown in Table 3, all youth behaviours were significant predictors, the strongest being openness to communication, Nagelkerke $R^2 = .27$. Youths' openness to communication increased the likelihood that the adolescents would view the family as democratic, and the other predictors decreased the likelihood. With a .75-cut off, the model correctly predicted 74.3% of the youths who reported their families to be undemocratic and 68.5% of those who reported their families to be democratic. The total correct prediction was 70%. In summary, then, information about youth characteristics seems to have about the same value as information about parental characteristics for predicting adolescents' judgments about the democratic climates in their families.

One could argue that these youths' behaviours are just products of parents' past or present treatment of the youth. If we were to use parents' behaviours as predictors of democracy, then, these youths' behaviours might not add anything. To test this, we used youths' and parents' behaviours as competing predictors (omitting parents' disclosure, which was not significant in the analysis of parent behaviours).

## Are youths' behaviours important, independent of parents' behaviours?

As shown in Table 4, both parents' warmth and parents' trust were significant predictors, warmth being the stronger of the two. Over and above that, however, both parents' and youths' reports of the youth's openness to communication were significant predictors. In fact, youth-reported openness to communication was the single most important predictor. The Nagelkerke $R^2$ was .34. The increase in prediction was significant when youths' characteristics were added to parents' characteristics as predictors (the increase in goodness-of-fit was 47.21, $df = 4$, $p < .001$). With a .75 cut-off, the overall model correctly predicted 71.5% of the youths who reported

TABLE 3

Logistic regression model predicting democratic versus undemocratic family climate from youths' behaviour

| Youth behaviour | Wald statistic | $p \leqslant$ |
| --- | --- | --- |
| Openness to communication (Y) | 51.26 | <.001 |
| Openness to communication (P) | 8.40 | .004 |
| Defiance (P) | 12.06 | .001 |
| Undesirable personality (Y) | 12.85 | .001 |

(Y) = youth-reported; (P) = parent-reported.

TABLE 4

Logistic regression model predicting democratic versus undemocratic family climate from parents' and youths' behaviours

| Behaviour | Wald statistic | $p \leqslant$ |
| --- | --- | --- |
| *Parent behaviour* | | |
| Trust (P) | 6.07 | .014 |
| Negative reactions (Y) | 2.31 | ns |
| Guilt induction (Y) | 0.72 | ns |
| Warmth (Y) | 17.12 | <.001 |
| *Youth behaviour* | | |
| Openness to communication (Y) | 27.35 | <.001 |
| Openness to communication (P) | 13.59 | <.001 |
| Defiance (P) | 3.99 | .046 |
| Undesirable personality (Y) | 3.31 | .069 |

(P) = parent-reported; (Y) = youth-reported.

their families to be undemocratic and 73.8% of those who reported their families to be democratic. The total correct prediction was 73.3%. As the random correct prediction with the given marginal frequencies was 56.5%, the improvement over chance was quite substantial (16.8%). We tested all of the two-way interactions between youths' and parents' behaviours, and none was significant. Thus, these results suggest that youths' behaviours—not just their responses to their parents' behaviours—are part of their conceptions of family democracy.

## DISCUSSION

In the literature on family climate in general and family democracy in particular, parents are assumed to be responsible for deciding the family climate. From this, one would expect that adolescents' judgments about whether or not their family is a democracy would be explained by their parents' behaviours alone. In this study, we found that they were not. Rather, adolescents' judgments of their families' government styles seemed to involve their own behaviours as well as those of their parents.

One might argue, however, that youths' behaviours are primarily products of parents' rearing practices early on, and thus bidirectional relations between adolescents' and parents' behaviours are not as bidirectional as they might seem, i.e., "much depends on the groundwork that was done in earlier years" (Maccoby, 1992, p. 183). But, this is to assume that parent-to-child influences are more unidirectional for younger children than for adolescents, and the literature does not bear that out. In fact, in the infancy literature, child effects on parents and interactions between parents' and children's behaviours are well established (e.g., Bates, Pettit, Dodge, & Ridge, 1998; Crockenberg & Leerkes, 2003, for a review; Seifer, Schiller, Sameroff, Resnick, & Riordan, 1996; Stattin & Klackenberg, 1992). Thus, there is no reason to dismiss the role that adolescents' behaviours play concurrently in their conceptualizations of family democracy on the grounds that adolescent behaviour is simply a product of earlier parenting.

Almost three out of four adolescents in this study considered their families to be democratic, and this is comparable to proportions found in other countries. In one Australian sample 63% of the families were classified democratic (Fallon & Bowles, 1998); in an American sample 83% of the adolescents perceived their parents to be democratic (Kelly & Goodwin, 1983); and studies on family decision making indicate that about 50% of family decisions are joint decisions in families with adolescents (Russell, Pettit, & Mize, 1998). Moreover, in a review on family relationships it was concluded that 75% of adolescents report having warm, pleasant relationships with their parents (Steinberg, 2001), and warmth was a strong predictor of democracy in this study. Overall, then, in agreement with previous studies, we find that the majority of adolescents seem to perceive their families to be democratic institutions.

Some limitations should be mentioned, however. First, families were categorized as democratic or undemocratic based on one question, even though the response options for that question gave rich descriptions of family interactions in different types of families. Second, this study has taken a cross-sectional look at these issues, but one would like to know how youths' perceptions of family democracy develop over time. In an ongoing study, we are collecting the data to look at these issues in longitudinal perspective. Finally, we have not dealt with gender, ethnicity, socioeconomic status, or structural aspects of the home, and these factors might moderate the relations that we have found, as they have moderated other family processes (Bumpus et al., 2001; Dornbusch, Ritter, Mont-Reynad, & Chen, 1990; Lamborn et al., 1996). However, in one study, decision-making style and adolescent academic performance were related even after gender, parent education, family structure, and ethnicity had been taken into account (Dornbusch et al., 1990). Whether our findings are independent of these factors is an empirical question.

What comes through in these findings, however, is that the democratic working of the family depends upon communication. Parents' warm, positive behaviour might be thought of as their openness to communication, making the adolescent feel loved, respected, and welcome to air opinions. However, adolescents' openness to communication, independent of parental warmth, seems to be essential in defining a democratic family climate, as well. Thus, openness from all sides seems to be important for family democracy.

Although more discussion in families with democratic climates is to be expected (Baldwin, 1948), this does not explain why youths' communication appears so important. This is consistent with what we have found previously, however. In a series of studies on how parents get knowledge about their youths' daily activities, we found that most of parents' knowledge comes from the youths themselves through their free, willing disclosure, rather than from parents' policing attempts (Kerr & Stattin, 2000; Kerr et al., 1999; Stattin & Kerr, 2000). Furthermore, parents' trust was largely dependent on how much information the youth freely supplied (Kerr et al., 1999). Thus, it appears that the information that adolescents provide about themselves and their activities are building blocks for a trusting relationship. In fact, one might question whether a democratic climate, where parents negotiate issues with their children, can exist if parents cannot trust their children and rely on the information they provide. From this line of argument, the democratic workings of the family cannot be fully described if adolescents' attempts to communicate are ignored as input to the family climate.

Here we have shown that an investigation of family democracy that asks questions about parents' behaviours will likely show that parents' behaviours are important. Similarly, an investigation that asks questions about youths' behaviours will show that youths' behaviours are important. The most accurate answer seems to be that both are important. We started with the question of whether adolescents themselves play a role in setting up the family climate. The answer seems to be yes. Clearly, parents are important, but adolescents are as well, particularly their willingness to make their parents part of their daily lives. Currently, from the most prominent literatures on parenting and adolescent adjustment (e.g., the monitoring and parenting-styles literatures), much of the advice to parents of adolescents is about setting rules and making sure that they are followed. Although this is undoubtedly important, new discoveries about parenting adolescents, and additional helpful advice to parents will likely involve ways to open up the channels of communication in the family.

# REFERENCES

Andershed, H., Kerr, M., Stattin, H., & Levander, S. (2002). Psychopathic traits in non-referred youths: A new assessment tool. In E. Blaauw & L. Sheridan (Eds.), *Psychopaths: Current international perspectives* (pp. 131–158). The Hague: Elsevier.

Anderson, K. E., Lytton, H., & Romney, D. M. (1986). Mothers' interactions with normal and conduct-disordered boys: Who affects whom? *Developmental Psychology, 22*, 604–609.

Baldwin, A. L. (1948). Socialization and the parent–child relationship. *Child Development, 19*, 127–136.

Baldwin, A. L. (1955). *Behavior and development in childhood*. New York: Dryden Press.

Bates, J. E., Pettit, G. S., Dodge, K. A., & Ridge, B. (1998). Interaction of temperamental resistance to control and restrictive parenting in the development of externalizing behaviour. *Developmental Psychology, 34*, 982–995.

Baumrind, D. (1968). Authoritarian vs. authoritative parental control. *Adolescence, 3*, 255–272.

Baumrind, D. (1991). Effective parenting during the early adolescent transition. In P. A. Cowan & E. M. Hetherington (Eds.), *Family transitions* (pp. 111–164). Hillsdale, NJ: Erlbaum.

Bell, R. Q., & Chapman, M. (1986). Child effects in studies using experimental or brief longitudinal approaches to socialization. *Developmental Psychology, 22*, 595–603.

Bloom, B. L. (1985). A factor analysis of self-report measures of family functioning. *Family Process, 24*, 225–239.

Bumpus, M. F., Crouter, A. C., & McHale, S. M. (2001). Parental autonomy granting during adolescence: Exploring gender differences in context. *Developmental Psychology, 37*, 163–173.

Crockenberg, S., & Leerkes, E. (2003). Infant negative emotionality, caregiving, and family relationships. In A. C. Crouter & A. Booth (Eds.), *Children's influence on family dynamics: The neglected side of family relationships* (pp. 57–78). Mahwah, NJ: Erlbaum.

Dix, T., Ruble, D. N., Grusec, J. E., & Nixon, S. (1986). Social cognition in parents: Inferential and affective reactions to children of three age levels. *Child Development, 57*, 879–894.

Dornbusch, S. M., Ritter, P. L., Mont-Reynad, R., & Chen, Z. (1990). Family decision making and academic performance in a diverse high school population. *Journal of Adolescent Research, 5*, 143–160.

Eccles, J. S., Buchanan, C. M., Flanagan, C., Fuligni, A., Midgley, C., & Yee, D. (1991). Control versus autonomy during early adolescence. *Journal of Social Issues, 47*, 53–68.

Fallon, B. J., & Bowles, T. V. P. (1998). Adolescents' influence and co-operation in family decision making. *Journal of Adolescence, 21*, 599–608.

Fuligni, A. J., & Eccles, J. S. (1993). Perceived parent–child relationships and early adolescents' orientation toward peers. *Developmental Psychology, 29*, 622–632.

Ge, X., Conger, R. D., Cadoret, R. J., Neiderhiser, J. M., Yates, W., Troughton, E., & Stewart, M. A. (1996). The developmental interface between nature and nurture: A mutual influence model of child antisocial behaviour and parent behaviours. *Developmental Psychology, 32*, 574–589.

Gray, M. R., & Steinberg, L. (1999). Unpacking authoritative parenting: Reassessing a multidimensional construct. *Journal of Marriage and the Family, 61*, 574–587.

Holmbeck, G. N., Paikoff, A., & Brooks-Gunn, J. (1995). Parenting adolescents. In M. Bornstein (Ed.), *The handbook of parenting* (Vol. 1, pp. 91–118). Mahwah, NJ: Erlbaum.

Kelly, C., & Goodwin, G. C. (1983). Adolescents' perception of three styles of parental control. *Adolescence, 18*, 567–571.

Kerr, M., & Stattin, H. (2000). What parents know, how they know it, and several forms of adolescent adjustment: Further evidence for a reinterpretation of monitoring. *Developmental Psychology, 36*, 366–380.

Kerr, M., & Stattin, H. (2003). Parenting of adolescents: Action or reaction? In A. C. Crouter & A. Booth (Eds.), *Children's influence on family dynamics: The neglected side of family relationships* (pp. 121–151). Mahwah, NJ: Lawrence Erlbaum Associates, Inc.

Kerr, M., Stattin, H., & Kiesner, J. (2004, February). *Peers and problem behaviour: Have we missed something?* Paper presented at the conference Hot Topics in Developmental Research: Peer Relationships in Adolescence, Nijmegen, the Netherlands.

Kerr, M., Stattin, H., & Trost, K. (1999). To know you is to trust you: Parents' trust is rooted in child disclosure of information. *Journal of Adolescence, 22*, 737–752.

Kim, K. J., Conger, R. D., Lorenz, F. O., & Elder, G. H., Jr. (2001). Parent–adolescent reciprocity in negative affect and its relation to early adult social development. *Developmental Psychology, 37*, 775–790.

Lamborn, S. D., Dornbusch, S. M., & Steinberg, L. (1996). Ethnicity and community context as moderators of the relations between family decision making and adolescent adjustment. *Child Development, 67*, 283–301.

Maccoby, E. E. (1992). Trends in the study of socialization: Is there a Lewinian heritage? *Journal of Social Issues, 48*, 171–185.

McHale, J. P., Kavanaugh, K. C., & Berkman, J. M. (2003). Sensitivity to infants' cues: As much a mandate for researchers as for parents. In A. C. Crouter & A. Booth (Eds.), *Children's influence on family dynamics: The neglected side of family relationships* (pp. 91–108). Mahwah, NJ: Lawrence Erlbaum Associates, Inc.

Neiderhiser, J. M., Reiss, D., Hetherington, E. M., & Plomin, R. (1999). Relationships between parenting and adolescent adjustment over time: Genetic and environmental contributions. *Developmental Psychology, 35*, 680–692.

Noller, P., Seth-Smith, M., Bouma, R., & Schweitzer, R. (1992). Parent and adolescent perceptions of family functioning: A comparison of clinic and nonclinic families. *Journal of Adolescence, 15*, 101–114.

Russell, A., Pettit, G. S., & Mize, J. (1998). Horizontal qualities in parent–child relationships: Parallels with and possible consequences for children's peer relationships. *Developmental Review, 18*, 313–352.

Seifer, R., Schiller, M., Sameroff, A. J., Resnick, S., & Riordan, K. (1996). Attachment, maternal sensitivity, and infant temperament during the first year of life. *Developmental Psychology, 12*–25.

Stattin, H., & Kerr, M. (2000). Parental monitoring: A reinterpretation. *Child Development, 71*, 1070–1083.

Stattin, H., & Klackenberg, G. (1992). Family discord in adolescence in the light of family discord in childhood: The maternal perspective. In W. Meeus, M. de Goede, W. Kox, & K. Hurrelman (Eds.), *Adolescence, careers, and cultures* (pp. 143–161). Berlin: de Gruyter.

Steinberg, L. (1990). Autonomy, conflict, and harmony in the family relationship. In S. S. Feldman & G. R. Elliott (Eds.), *At the threshold: The developing adolescent* (pp. 255–276). Cambridge, MA: Harvard University Press.

Steinberg, L. (2001). We know some things: Parent–adolescent relationships in retrospect and prospect. *Journal of Research on Adolescence, 11*, 1–19.

Steinberg, L., Mounts, N. S., Lamborn, S. D., & Dornbusch, S. M. (1991). Authoritative parenting and adolescent adjustment across varied ecological niches. *Journal of Research on Adolescence, 1*, 19–36.

Teti, D. M., & Gelfland, D. M. (1991). Behavioural competence among mothers and infants in the first year: The mediational role of maternal self-efficacy. *Child Development, 62*, 918–929.

van den Boom, C. D., & Hoeksma, J. B. (1994). The effect of infant irritability on mother–infant interaction: A growth curve analysis. *Developmental Psychology, 30*, 581–590.

EUROPEAN JOURNAL OF DEVELOPMENTAL PSYCHOLOGY, 2004, *1*(4), 331–348

# Personality type, social relationships, and problem behaviour in adolescence

Marcel A. G. van Aken and Judith Semon Dubas

*Utrecht University, The Netherlands*

In a number of recent studies on personality in childhood and adolescence, comparable personality types have been distinguished. The three types that are repeatedly found can be labelled as: *resilient, overcontrolled,* and *undercontrolled.* Using data from a short-term longitudinal study of 569 adolescents, we investigated the transactions between type membership and perceived family and peer support and coercion in predicting problem behaviour, and the concomitants of stability and change in type membership. Resilients report the most perceived support from family members and from friends and the lowest parental coercion. Overcontrollers and undercontrollers report similarly low levels of support and undercontrollers report the highest amount of parental coercion. The types also differ in their psychosocial functioning, with overcontrollers and undercontrollers showing more internalizing and social problems and undercontrollers additionally showing more externalizing problems. Interactions between type and support in predicting the level of problem behaviour were found; support seemed more relevant for over-controllers, and coercion more for resilients and undercontrollers. Type membership was moderately stable over a period of three years, a stability that in several instances seems to be related to perceived relational support and to problem behaviour.

In this paper, we focus on the transactions between adolescents' personality organization on the one hand and the social relationships that surround them on the other. More specifically, we present data on the social relationships of three personality types and on the way that type member-ship and relationships interact in determining psychosocial functioning in adolescence. We also study various developmental patterns of stability and change of personality type during adolescence, and the antecedents and consequences of these developmental patterns.

Correspondence should be addressed to Marcel A. G. van Aken, Department of Developmental Psychology, Utrecht University, PO Box 80.140, NL-3508 TC Utrecht, The Netherlands. E-mail: m.a.g.vanaken@fss.uu.nl

© 2004 Psychology Press Ltd

http://www.tandf.co.uk/journals/pp/17405629.html    DOI: 10.1080/17405620444000166

## Personality types

Recently, several studies have found three replicable personality types in children and adolescents. These studies either formed these types using Q-factor analyses on Block and Block's (1980) California Child Q-set (Robins, John, Caspi, Moffitt, Stouthamer-Loeber, 1996; Hart, Hofman, Edelstein, & Keller, 1997; Asendorpf & Van Aken, 1999) or other statistical procedures, such as cluster analysis (Asendorpf, Borkenau, Ostendorpf, & Van Aken, 2001; Caspi & Silva, 1995; Dubas, Gerris, Janssens, & Vermulst, 2002; Newman, Caspi, Moffitt, & Silva, 1997; Van Aken, Van Lieshout, Scholte, & Haselager, 2002; Scholte, Van Lieshout, De Wit, & Van Aken, in press; Harrington, Chin, Rickey, & Mohr, 1999) or configural frequency analysis (Aksan et al., 1999).

The first type is characterized by a high level of ego-resiliency and a moderate level of ego-control. In addition, this type scores high on all of the five FFM-dimensions. This type is labelled the *resilients*. A second type is characterized by a low level of ego-resiliency combined with a high level of ego-control (in the direction of overcontrol). In addition, this type scores low on extraversion and emotional stability, high on agreeableness and conscientiousness, and moderate on openness. This type is labelled the *overcontrollers*. A third type is characterized by a low level of ego-resiliency combined with a low level of ego-control. In addition, this type has low levels of agreeableness, conscientiousness and openness, low to moderate scores on emotional stability and moderate to high scores on extraversion. This type is labelled the *undercontrollers*.

## Psychosocial functioning of the three types

Several studies showed that the three personality types have a distinct pattern of psychosocial and relational functioning (for a review see Van Aken et al., 2002). The resilients seem to function well in all domains. Compared to the other two types, they perform better in school, show less behaviour and emotional problems, and have good relationships with parents and peers. Undercontrollers seem to have more externalizing problems, such as antisocial behaviour and higher levels of aggression, and they report lower levels of support from parents and from peers. Overcontrollers seem to have more internalizing problems, such as social withdrawal and low self-esteem. They also report lower levels of support from parents and from peers.

It is important to realize that these results are on a group level, that is, not all undercontrollers show externalizing behaviours and not all overcon-trollers show internalizing behaviours. Our hypothesis is that it is the combination of personality type and the quality of their social relationships that puts an adolescent at risk. Recent studies on the interplay between personality, relationships, and developmental outcomes point towards the importance of considering person–environment transactions in studying these processes (Caspi, 2000).

In one of the few investigations of personality–environment transactions among adolescents, O'Connor and Dvorak (2001) found that parenting behaviours moderated the link between resiliency and anxiety, delinquency and aggression for both males and females. In addition, maternal control moderated the link between resiliency and depression for females. For highly resilient individuals the associations between parenting and outcomes were essentially zero, whereas for the less resilient groups there were various associations. Also, a transaction was found between maternal harshness and aggression for males. Among the low resilient males, maternal harshness was associated with higher levels of aggression.

A replication and extension of these latter findings was recently found in a national sample of Dutch adolescents (Dubas, Gerris, Janssens, & Vermulst, 2002). In this study, parenting practices (i.e., restrictive control and positive control) moderated the association between personality type and problem behaviours. Undercontrollers from highly restrictive families were more likely to experience high levels of depressive affect, moodiness and internalizing problems than their counterparts in less restrictive families. These findings are consistent with those of O'Connor and Dvorak (2001) who found that individuals who were low on resiliency were particularly vulnerable to parenting behaviours and extend it by identifying the fact that these "less resilient" individuals are most likely undercontrollers and not overcontrollers who are most vulnerable to harsh parenting.

These results suggest that personality type by parenting transactions should be detected in the present study. Undercontrollers and overcontrollers may be more sensitive to the types of relationships that they have with family members than resilients. In addition to the role that parents may play in moderating the relation between personality type and adjustment, friendships and peer relations at this time may also be important.

In an earlier study, Van Aken et al. (2002) tested transactions between personality type and peer relationships (operationalized in terms of sociometric scores) among Dutch adolescents. Several significant transactions were found with measures of psychosocial adjustment as outcome variables. For overcontrollers, an effect was found on loneliness: only disliked overcontrollers reported more loneliness than liked overcontrollers did, for resilients and undercontrollers the subtypes did not differ. For undercontrollers, effects were found on covert antisocial behaviour: disliked undercontrollers showed more antisocial behaviour than liked undercontrollers did, whereas no differences were found between liked and disliked resilients or overcontrollers.

In the present paper, we extend these investigations in two ways. First, we study transactions not only with peer relations (in terms of perceived friend support and coercion) but also with family relations (perceived family support and coercion) and, second, we investigate personality type main effects and transactions in a longitudinal design. Our focus is on whether having supportive relationships with family or friends serves as a means of moderating the developmental relations between personality type and psychosocial functioning.

## Aims of this paper

After examining the main effects of adolescent personality types on psychosocial adjustment and the quality of relationships with parents and peers, in this paper we study Personality Type × Relationship transactions. Our hypotheses are that psychosocial adjustment is the result of the interplay between personality and environment, so that including relationship variables specifies the effects of personality on psychosocial adjustment. More specifically, we expect that perceived family and friend support, and family and friend coercion moderate the effects of personality on psychosocial functioning: overcontrollers and undercontrollers with high perceived support and low coercion are expected to function better in a number of psychosocial domains than those with low perceived support and high coercion. In addition, we study the stability and change of type membership over a period of three years. Our hypothesis is that stability and change in personality type is related to the initial level as well as the development of the quality of relationships and psychosocial functioning during adolescence.

## METHOD

### Sample

Participants were drawn from the *Nijmegen Family and Personality Study*, a short-term longitudinal study of parents with adolescent children (Haselager & Van Aken, 1999) that began in 1997 and followed 288 families once annually for three measurement waves. The participants included mothers, fathers, and two adolescent siblings who completed a diverse battery of psychological and sociological measures designed to assess individual characteristics of parents and children as well as the family as a whole. There were 68 boy–boy (23.6%), 76 girl–girl (26.4%), 76 boy–girl (26.4%) and 68 girl–boy (23.6%) sibling pairs. In the first measurement wave, the oldest children were on average 14.6 years ($SD = 10$ months) and the youngest children were on average 12.4 years ($SD = 9$ months). The sample represents middle to upper middle class Dutch families in terms of income and educational level. The final sample of the present study consisted of 569 adolescents with complete personality data for the analyses at wave 1, or 545 adolescents who had complete data on all measures across all 3 waves for the longitudinal analyses.

## Procedure

Eligible families were identified and recruited from 23 municipal civil registers in the Netherlands. To be included in the sample, both parents and at least two biological adolescent children (between the ages of 11 and 15 years of age) were to be living at the same address. Families were sent letters describing the study and inviting them to participate. After written consent had been obtained, an appointment for a home visit was made. Trained interviewers visited the home and distributed questionnaire packets to each family member. Parents and the two children completed a set of questionnaires designed to tap a variety of psychological, social and emotional characteristics including close relationships, problem behaviour, and personality. Families who had participated all three times were eligible for five lottery prizes consisting of 2000 guilders each (approximately $800). Attrition rate was very low: of the 288 families that started the study, 285 were still participating in wave 3.

## Measures

*Personality.*  A Dutch adaptation (Gerris, Houtmans, Kwaaitaal-Roosen, Schipper, Vermulst, & Janssens, 1998) of 30 adjective big-five personality markers selected from Goldberg (1992) was used to assess adolescents' self-reports on personality characteristics. The questionnaire consists of 30 seven-point items and operationalizes five dimensions, i.e., *extraversion* (e.g., talkative), *conscientiousness* (e.g., systematic), *agreeableness* (e.g., helpful), *emotional stability* (e.g., nervous), and *openness to experience* (e.g., innovative). Cronbach alphas computed for each of the personality dimensions were satisfactory and ranged from .63 to .89.

*Behavioural, emotional and social problems.*  The *problem behaviour list* (PBL; De Bruyn, Vermulst, & Scholte, 2003) was used to obtain parent reports on children's behavioural/emotional problems. The questionnaire consists of 30 items by means of which the parent can indicate to what extent each item is true for each of the two children on a 5-point scale. Scores for two broadband groups of syndromes *internalizing* and *externalizing* can be computed. Internalizing consists of the *anxious* and *withdrawn* subscales. Externalizing consists of the *aggressive* and *delinquent behaviour* subscales. An additional subscale labelled *social problems* was used in the present study as an index of the extent to which the adolescent is not accepted by others and prefers to be alone. To compute a problem score for the children, the ratings from mother and father for a child were combined (alphas ranged from .81 to .90).

*Relational support from family and friends.* The *relational support inventory* (RSI; Scholte, Van Lieshout, & Van Aken, 2001) was used to measure the support that children receive from their parents, siblings, and a best friend. This self-report questionnaire is composed of 27 five-point items and operationalizes five relational support dimensions: *emotional support* (e.g., "This person shows me that he/she loves me"); *respect for autonomy* (e.g., "This person lets me decide as often as possible"); *quality of information* (e.g., "This person explains to me how I can make or do something"); *convergence of goals* (e.g., "This person and I have the same opinions about use of drugs, alcohol, or gambling"); and *acceptance* (e.g., "This person accepts me as I am"). These subscales were combined to form a scale *perceived family support* (average support perceived from father, mother, and sibling, aggregated over the five dimensions), and *perceived friend support* (average support perceived from best friend, aggregated over the five dimensions). Alphas for family support in the first measurement wave for oldest children were .85 for support from mother, .87 for support from father and .85 for support from sibling; for the youngest children, these alphas were .80, .80 and .86, respectively. For friend support, alphas were .74 for the youngest children and .72 for the oldest children.

*Coercion from parents, siblings and friends.* A six-item scale adapted from the work of Howard, Blumstein, & Schwartz (1986) was used to measure the degree to which family members and friends used negative (coercive) means to get the child to do something he or she did not wish to do (e.g., "threatens me" or "insults me"). Adolescents rated each parent, a sibling and best friend separately. Mean rating across family members were used to calculate family coercion and the friend score was used for friend coercion. Alphas ranged from .80 to .92.

## Derivation of the personality types

Time 1 personality types were derived using *k*-means cluster analysis with three factors set as the number of factors based on previous findings that three main types (resilients, overcontrollers, undercontrollers) have been found and replicated in a variety of samples including Dutch adolescents

(Scholte et al., in press). Because our data are drawn from a relatively small, homogenous sample of, generally speaking, well functioning families (none are divorced and all have been together for at least fifteen years) we used a priori cluster centres derived from previous work on personality types and the big five. Prior to the first set of cluster analyses all personality dimension scores were converted to $z$-scores within the two target children groups— oldest children and youngest children. We created the clusters separately for older and younger siblings. We then compared the final cluster centres for each of the types and found no significant differences.

The fact that the final cluster centres were virtually identical is in our opinion one testimony to the replicability of the types. As a second check on the replicability of the types we randomly divided the youngest and oldest child samples in half, derived the clusters and compared the cluster centres and the classifications of individuals across these two types. Again no differences within the age groups were found. As a third check on replicability we created a sample of adolescents in which either the oldest or youngest child was randomly selected to be the target child and conducted the cluster analyses on only one child per family. Results were again virtually the same. Finally, we also created types with no a priori cluster centres and compared these cluster centres to those based on a priori clustering. Results revealed that the cluster labelled undercontrollers were higher on agreeableness than would have been expected. The congruence in type classification was still fairly high with kappa coefficients .68 for the oldest children and .61 for the youngest children. Thus, we were reasonably confident that our a priori types were replicable.

Time 2 and Time 3 personality types were derived using the Time 1 final cluster centres (raw scores) as the initial cluster centres. Again these were calculated separately for youngest and oldest children. There was little difference in cluster centres across time. In this sample of 569 adolescents,[1] we found 36% resilients, 28% overcontrollers and 36% undercontrollers at Time 1 with similar distributions for the subsequent waves. There was a fairly equal distribution of gender within the resilients (51.5% girls), but

---

[1]We recognize that we might have problems of dependency in that 50% of the children are from the same family and reporting on their relational support about the same parents and that also the parent reports on problem behaviour are also dependent in that the parents provide reports on two children. It should be noted that we also conducted all second phase analyses (i.e., those that examine correlates of the types) on a sample of adolescents in which only one child per family was randomly selected. Results from this random sample were virtually the same as the full sample. We used the full sample in order to ensure sufficient statistical power for our analyses involving identifying factors related to stability and change in types across adolescence.

there were slightly more girls among the overcontrollers (58.4%) and slightly more boys among the undercontrollers (54.4%).

# RESULTS

## Concurrent differences between the types

Our first set of analyses focused on verifying whether there were behavioural and social relationship differences among the types at Time 1. We ran a preliminary ANOVA checking whether there were age differences among the three types. Results revealed significant age differences, $F(2, 560) = 4.42$, $p < .001$. Tukey post-hoc tests revealed that undercontrollers (mean age = 13.3 years) were significantly younger than overcontrollers (mean age = 13.7 years), with resilients intermediate (mean age = 13.5 years). All subsequent analyses were run with and without age as a covariate. The results were virtually identical whether or not age was included in the model.

We ran two sets of multivariate analysis of variance (MANOVA) examining whether there were differences among the types, one that focused on the internalizing, externalizing and social problems and the other that focused on family and friend support and coercion. We report results in which age was not included in the model. Significant effects were followed up with Tukey post-hoc tests. Because significant gender differences in internalizing and externalizing behaviour have been reported among adolescents we also ran these analyses including gender as a between-subjects factor. Although main effects of gender on externalizing and social problems were found (in both cases boys > girls), and on friend support (girls > boys) there were no Gender × Type interactions. Therefore, we did not include gender in the model for the results reported here.

As in earlier studies, resilients were found to have the lowest scores on problem behaviour (in this study reported by their parents). Overcontrollers were described as having more internalizing problems and more social problems than resilients, but scored the same on externalizing problems. Undercontrollers scored higher than resilients on social problems, and the same as resilients on externalizing problems, but higher than overcontrollers on externalizing problems. They also scored higher than resilients on internalizing problems. Both overcontrollers and undercontrollers reported similarly low family and friend support and high coercion. We also ran repeated measures MANOVAs in order to examine whether these results remained over time. No Type × Time interactions on problem behaviour were found, indicating that the differences in problem behaviour between the three types, which already existed at Time 1, did not change over the subsequent measurement waves. There was a significant Type × Time interaction on the support variables and family coercion; results from follow-up analysis of this interaction indicated that the main effect of type lessened over time.

## The role of relationships in moderating the effects of personality type on problem behaviours

Our next set of analyses was designed to examine whether having either high or low levels of support or coercion moderated the effect of personality type on problem behaviours. Drawing from the finding that resilients, by definition, are high in ego resiliency and less prone to problem behaviours we predicted that level of support or coercion either from parents or friends would not be related to any of the problem behaviours (internalizing, externalizing and social problems). For overcontrollers and undercontrollers we predicted that family and friend support might help to diminish any negative behavioural "consequences" (correlates) type membership may have.

Our first step in this analysis was to classify individuals into high and low levels of relationship quality. Our classifications were done separately for family and friend support and also for family and friend coercion. Hence any given individual may be classified as high on one variable but not high on the other. We used the median to split the family and friend relationship variables into high and low levels and classified adolescents as having high support if they were at or above the median and as having low support if they were below the median.

We conducted four 3 (personality type) × 2 (support group, high or low) MANOVAs on the problem behaviour variables. In the first we examined the role of family support, in the second friend support, in the third family coercion and in the fourth friend coercion. For these analyses we only used the wave 1 data. A significant multivariate interaction effect for friend coercion and personality types was found along with marginal multivariate interaction effects for both family support, friend support, and family coercion with personality types. These overall tests were followed by planned comparisons to test the effects of support for each of the personality types.

Table 1 shows some evidence of personality Type × Family Support interactions: for social problems, overcontrollers with high family support had lower problem scores than overcontrollers with low family support. This was marginally the case for undercontrollers but not for the resilients. For externalizing problems a clear main effect of family support was found, for all three types.

Somewhat more clearer evidence for personality Type × Friend Support interactions was found: on all three problem domains, overcontrollers with high friend support scored lower than overcontrollers with low friend

TABLE 1
Contrasts on adjustment using friend and family support levels to make subtypes of
overcontrollers, undercontrollers and resilients (wave 1 data only)

| | Externalizing | Internalizing | Social problems |
|---|---|---|---|
| *Resilients* | | | |
| High family support ($N = 135$) | 1.50 | 1.88 | 1.69 |
| Low family support ($N = 70$) | 1.64 | 1.94 | 1.80 |
| *t*-value | 2.65** | 0.84 | 1.41 |
| *Overcontrollers* | | | |
| High family support ($N = 76$) | 1.43 | 2.05 | 1.77 |
| Low family support ($N = 81$) | 1.58 | 2.18 | 1.94 |
| *t*-value | 2.47* | 1.64 | 2.06* |
| *Undercontrollers* | | | |
| High family support ($N = 70$) | 1.52 | 2.04 | 1.81 |
| Low family support ($N = 131$) | 1.68 | 2.13 | 1.95 |
| *t*-value | 2.75** | 1.20 | 1.85[+] |
| | | | |
| *Resilients* | | | |
| High friend support ($N = 130$) | 1.52 | 1.88 | 1.71 |
| Low friend support ($N = 64$) | 1.61 | 1.93 | 1.78 |
| *t*-value | 1.50 | 0.66 | 1.04 |
| *Overcontrollers* | | | |
| High friend support ($N = 75$) | 1.44 | 2.05 | 1.76 |
| Low friend support ($N = 72$) | 1.57 | 2.19 | 1.96 |
| *t*-value | 2.05* | 1.73[+] | 2.51* |
| *Undercontrollers* | | | |
| High friend support ($N = 71$) | 1.62 | 2.09 | 1.83 |
| Low friend support ($N = 125$) | 1.62 | 2.11 | 1.95 |
| *t*-value | 0.06 | 0.25 | 1.57 |

[+] $p < .10$; * $p < .05$; ** $p < .01$; *** $p < .001$.

support, whereas for undercontrollers and resilients there were not even tendencies towards such an effect.

Table 2 shows that for family coercion, resilients with low family coercion scored lower on all three problem behaviours than resilients with high family coercion. For overcontrollers there was no effect of family coercion. For undercontrollers the effects of family coercion were even more striking than that for resilients: undercontrollers with high family coercion scored higher on all problem behaviours than undercontrollers with low family coercion.

For friend coercion, resilients with low friend coercion scored lower on internalizing and externalizing problem behaviours than resilients with high friend coercion. Similar to family coercion, there was no effect of friend coercion for overcontrollers. Finally, for undercontrollers the effects of friend coercion were in the same direction as family coercion: undercontrollers with high friend coercion scored higher on all problem behaviours than undercontrollers with low friend coercion.

## TABLE 2
Contrasts on adjustment using friend and family coercion levels to make subtypes of overcontrollers, undercontrollers and resilients (wave 1 data only)

|  | Externalizing | Internalizing | Social problems |
|---|---|---|---|
| *Resilients* |  |  |  |
| Low family coercion ($N = 133$) | 1.49 | 1.83 | 1.67 |
| High family coercion ($N = 71$) | 1.63 | 2.03 | 1.83 |
| *t*-value | − 2.62** | − 3.10** | − 2.46** |
| *Overcontrollers* |  |  |  |
| Low family coercion ($N = 76$) | 1.47 | 2.07 | 1.82 |
| High family coercion ($N = 80$) | 1.54 | 2.15 | 1.90 |
| *t*-value | − 1.30 ns | − 1.16 ns | − 0.98 ns |
| *Undercontrollers* |  |  |  |
| Low family coercion ($N = 89$) | 1.51 | 1.90 | 1.75 |
| High family coercion ($N = 112$) | 1.70 | 2.25 | 2.02 |
| *t*-value | − 3.60*** | − 4.65** | − 3.85*** |
| *Resilients* |  |  |  |
| Low friend coercion ($N = 142$) | 1.50 | 1.85 | 1.70 |
| High friend coercion ($N = 61$) | 1.65 | 2.02 | 1.79 |
| *t*-value | − 2.74** | − 2.54* | − 0.98 ns |
| *Overcontrollers* |  |  |  |
| Low friend coercion ($N = 89$) | 1.49 | 2.12 | 1.82 |
| High friend coercion ($N = 66$) | 1.53 | 2.10 | 1.89 |
| *t*-value | − 0.82 ns | − 0.14 ns | − 0.94 ns |
| *Undercontrollers* |  |  |  |
| Low friend coercion ($N = 107$) | 1.55 | 1.97 | 1.80 |
| High friend coercion ($N = 94$) | 1.69 | 2.25 | 2.01 |
| *t*-value | − 2.69** | − 3.72*** | − 2.72** |

$^{+}p < .10$; $^{*}p < .05$; $^{**}p < .01$; $^{***}p < .001$; ns = not significant.

## TABLE 3
Stability of type membership across time

| Cross-time personality type | N |
|---|---|
| Pure resilients (RRR) | 83 |
| Pure overcontrollers (OOO) | 58 |
| Pure undercontrollers (UUU) | 66 |
| Fallen resilients to overcontrollers (ROO or RRO) | 19 |
| Fallen resilients to undercontrollers (RUU or RRU) | 61 |
| Saved overcontrollers (OOR or ORR) | 42 |
| Saved undercontrollers (UUR or URR) | 37 |

## Stability of personality types

The next step in our analysis was to examine the stability of type membership across time. Table 3 provides the breakout of types across time, in which we presented those types that showed a specific pattern of either stability (that is, the three types that were the same across all three measurement waves), improvement (defined as becoming classified as a resilient), or decline (defined as changing from a resilient to either an overcontroller or undercontroller).

Over the three measurement waves 38% of the children were stable, 15% decreased from being a resilient to either being an overcontroller (4%) or an undercontroller (11%), 14% improved towards being a resilient from being either an overcontroller (8%) or an undercontroller (7%), and the remaining 33% showed random movement.

We tested the stability of the personality types over the three measurement waves with a *configural frequency analysis* (CFA, performed with the Sleipner-software, Version 2.0, Bergman & El-Khouri, 1998). Tests were made for types (configurations that occur significantly more often as expected) and antitypes (configurations that occur significantly less often as expected).

Of the 27 possible combinations (three types, three waves) five significant types emerged. Among those five were the three "stable" types, the stable resilients (83 out of 545 subjects [15%], $\chi^2 = 144.69$, $p < .00001$), the stable overcontrollers (58 out of 545 [11%], $\chi^2 = 130.37$, $p < .00001$), and the stable undercontrollers (66 out of 545 [12%], $\chi^2 = 81.96$, $p < .00001$). In addition to these stable types, we also found a type that consisted of adolescents who were resilient in the first measurement wave, but under-controlled in the second and third (44 out of 545 [8%], $\chi^2 = 19.44$, $p < .001$) and a small but significant type that consisted of adolescents who were undercontrolled in the first measurement wave but overcontrolled in the second and third (38 out of 545 [7%], $\chi^2 = 18.84$, $p < .01$). In addition to these types, we found seven antitypes that mostly consisted of a combination of a different type in every wave.

## Antecedents and consequences of the longitudinal personality types

The next step in our analyses was to examine how the longitudinal personality types were related to both the problem behaviour and relational support variables across the three waves of measurement. We compared the pure type to its concomitant saved or fallen counterpart (pure resilients to fallen resilients, pure overcontrollers to saved overcontrollers, pure under-

## TABLE 4
### Psychosocial functioning of the stable and changing types

| | Resilients | | | | Overcontrollers | | | Undercontrollers | | |
|---|---|---|---|---|---|---|---|---|---|---|
| | Pure (n = 83) | to UC (n = 61) | to OC (n = 19) | F | pure (n = 58) | saved (n = 42) | F | pure (n = 37) | saved (n = 37) | F |
| Intern. | 1.83 | 1.87 | 1.90 | 0.42 | 2.18 | 1.98 | 5.04* | 2.05 | 1.93 | 1.43 |
| Extern. | 1.49 | 1.58 | 1.50 | 1.70 | 1.50 | 1.48 | 0.15 | 1.66 | 1.51 | 3.83[+] |
| Soc. | 1.61 | 1.71 | 1.70 | 1.37 | 1.88 | 1.69 | 4.69* | 1.88 | 1.63 | 7.11** |
| FamSup | 4.35[a] | 4.02[b] | 4.08[ab] | 17.87*** | 3.96 | 4.11 | 5.46* | 3.90 | 4.11 | 2.50 |
| FriSup | 4.39[a] | 4.25[b] | 4.23[b] | 5.23* | 4.12 | 4.20 | 1.98 | 4.07 | 4.06 | 0.07 |
| FamCoer | 1.25[a] | 1.40[b] | 1.51[ab] | 11.09*** | 1.51 | 1.39 | 2.49 | 1.56 | 1.48 | 0.68 |
| FriCoer | 1.19[a] | 1.20[b] | 1.17[a] | 4.42* | 1.28 | 1.26 | 0.24 | 1.35 | 1.31 | 0.01 |

*Note.* Means are aggregated over waves, there were no time × type interactions, except on friend coercion. For the resilient subtypes, different superscripts indicate that the groups differed significantly. [+] $p = .056$; * $p < .05$; ** $p < .01$; *** $p < .001$.

343

controllers to saved undercontrollers). We used repeated measures ANOVA with Tukey post-hoc tests to analyse longitudinal differences among the groups on family and friend support and coercion, internalizing, externalizing and social problems.

Table 4 shows the results of the comparison between the stable personality types and their changing counterparts. For the comparisons of pure resilients to fallen resilients, four significant differences emerged. Fallen resilients to undercontrollers reported lower family support and higher family and friend coercion than pure resilients. Fallen resilients to overcontrollers, in most cases, were intermediate. Both kinds of fallen resilients reported lower friend support. There was a Type × Time interaction, $F(2, 139) = 3.06$, $p = .05$ on friend coercion with results indicating that the gap between the pure resilients and fallen resilients to undercontrollers increased across time.

For overcontrollers there were significant differences among the types on both internalizing and social problems. Pure overcontrollers reported higher levels of problems than saved overcontrollers did. In addition, there were significant differences between the two types on family support. Pure overcontrollers reported lower levels of family support than saved overcontrollers did. There were no Type × Time interactions, nor were there differences among the groups on friend support, on family or friend coercion, or on externalizing behaviours.

For undercontrollers there was a significant difference among the types on social problems, and a trend towards a significant difference on externalizing problems. In both cases, saved undercontrollers reported lower levels of problems than pure undercontrollers did. There were no differences on family and friend support or coercion, and again there were no Type × Time interactions.

## DISCUSSION

The present investigation identified three replicable personality types that have consistently been found in several previous investigations that examined children, adolescents or adults (Asendorpf et al., 2001). Earlier reported differences between the types in their psychosocial functioning were also confirmed. Resilients clearly showed the highest levels of psychosocial functioning and of perceived family and friend support. When compared to the other two types, overcontrollers were rated by their parents higher on having social problems and having internalizing problems, undercontrollers as higher on having social problems and having externalizing problems. The unexpected finding that undercontrollers were also rated as higher than resilients on internalizing problems probably points to a comorbidity of both kinds of problems in this sample. This comorbidity may exist either on the group level (some undercontrollers have externalizing problems, some have internalizing problems) or at the individual level (undercontrollers have both externalizing and internalizing problems). It is not clear whether this comorbidity can be attributed to characteristics of this specific sample. Although our attrition rate was very low, it could be the case that given that the subjects in this study were from intact, two-parent families that agreed at the onset to participate over three consecutive years, more problematic families (or the families with more problematic children) did not participate in the study from the start.

We were partly able to replicate the Personality Type × Relationship interactions that were found earlier (Van Aken et al., 2002; Dubas et al., 2002; O'Connor & Dvorak, 2001). We found several instances of an interaction between personality type and social relationships in predicting problem behaviour. A differential pattern emerged where family and friend support seems especially relevant for overcontrollers, whereas family and friend coercion seem important for resilients and undercontrollers. Overcontrollers perceiving high family or friend support were reported by parents as having less problem behaviour, whereas this did not seem to matter for resilients and undercontrollers. On the other hand, resilients and undercontrollers experiencing higher family and friend coercion were reported by parents as having more problem behaviour, while coercion did not seem to matter for overcontrollers' adjustment. These results seem to point to a differential effect of social relationships with parents and friends: the supportive elements seem particularly salient for overcontrollers, whereas the coercive elements matter more for resilients and under-controllers. Although Dubas et al. did not examine coercion, they did find that undercontrollers receiving restrictive parenting experienced more problems.

A unique aspect of this study is that we also examined the stability of personality type membership across time. Our results suggest that both continuity and change in personality types are possible. In our sample only about one-third of the sample was classified as stable, another third showed a clear direction, in that they either improved or worsened and the remaining third exhibited random movement. It should be noted that the percentage stable that we reported should be considered as a lower bound: within the group of random movers, there are subjects who were of the same type at the beginning and at the end, but differed in between. If these subjects are considered as "weakly stable" the percentage of more or less stable subjects increases to 49%.

This finding is consistent with much of the research that has taken a variable-centred approach to personality, which has found that stability in most personality characteristics is not found until about age 30 (McCrae &

Costa, 1994). In a recent meta-analysis of the rank – order consistency of personality traits, Roberts and DelVecchio (2000) reported an estimated population correlation of .47 for the adolescent period (age 12 – 17.9). Our study suggests that even using a person-centred approach, stability during adolescence, particularly mid-adolescence, is moderate to low. These results are consistent with Asendorpf and Van Aken's (1999) work on the stability of types among children—where the stability of type membership between age 4 – 6 and age 10 was also moderate to low.

Although we found the developmental patterns of undercontrollers and overcontrollers to be related to their problem behaviour and their relational support and coercion, the results thus far do not give a clear indication of the causal direction. Pure resilients reported higher levels of family and friend support than changing resilients (in either direction), but did not differ from them in terms of their problem behaviour. Saved overcontrollers reported higher levels of family support than did pure overcontrollers, and at the same time their parents reported lower initial levels of internalizing and social problems for these children compared to parents of pure overcontrollers. Pure undercontrollers did not differ from saved under-controllers in terms of family and friend support and coercion, but were reported as having more social problems and (a trend towards) more externalizing problems. Thus, even though several of the analyses indicate differences in social relations or in problem behaviour between the stable types and their changing counterparts, the lack of interactions with time imply that it is still not possible to tease apart whether these changes in social relations and problem behaviours are being evoked, are causing or are bidirectional. Moreover, the findings differ by personality type. The fact that differences in social relations exist, even when behaviour problems do not yet differentiate the subtypes, nonetheless underscores the reciprocal interplay of personality and the social context. It may be more that this reciprocal dynamic is not being captured when measured at one-year intervals.

The present study attempted to investigate person – environment transactions during adolescence and how such transactions over-time may lead to change or stability in personality type. Whereas we examined the separate influence that friend and family may play in individual development, the combination of peer and family support together with the kind of peers who are providing the support may be what is most critical. Low levels of family support coupled with high levels of support from deviant peers may pull the adolescent down into a "fallen" path. Alternatively, low levels of family support but high levels of friend support with non-deviant peers may help to "save" one's disposition. Further work concerning the identification of antecedents and consequences of type membership is clearly needed. The present study highlights the importance of the family and peer contexts as two arenas in which these future studies should invest.

# REFERENCES

Aksan, N., Goldsmith, H. H., Smider, N. A., Essex, M. J., Clark, R., Hyde, J. S., Klein, M. H., & Vandell, D. L. (1999). Derivation and prediction of temperamental types among preschoolers. *Developmental Psychology, 35,* 958–971.

Asendorpf, J. B., Borkenau, P., Ostendorf, F., & Van Aken, M. A. G. (2001). Carving personality description at its joints: Confirmation of three replicable personality prototypes for both children and adults. *European Journal of Personality, 15,* 169–198.

Asendorpf, J. B., & Van Aken, M. A. G. (1999). Resilient, overcontrolled and undercontrolled personality prototypes in childhood: Replicability, predictive power, and the trait/type issue. *Journal of Personality and Social Psychology, 77,* 815–832.

Bergman, L. P., & El-Khouri, B. M. (1998). *Sleipner: A statistical package for pattern-oriented analysis, Vs. 2.* Stockholm: Stockholm University, Department of Psychology.

Block, J. H., & Block, J. (1980). The role of ego-control and ego-resiliency in the organization of behaviour. In W. A. Collins (Ed.), *Minnesota symposium on child psychology* (Vol. 13, pp. 39–101). Hillsdale, NJ: Lawrence Erlbaum Associates, Inc.

Caspi, A. (2000). The child is the father of the man: Personality continuities from childhood to adulthood. *Journal of Personality and Social Psychology, 78,* 158–172.

Caspi, A., & Silva, P. A. (1995). Temperamental qualities at age three predict personality traits in young adulthood: Longitudinal evidence from a birth cohort. *Child Development, 66,* 486–498.

De Bruyn, E. E. J., Vermulst, A. A., & Scholte, R. H. J. (2003). *The Nijmegen problem behaviour list: Construction and psychometric characteristics* (manuscript submitted for publication).

Dubas, J. S., Gerris, J. R. M., Janssens, J. M. A. M., & Vermulst, A. A. (2002). Personality types of adolescents: Concurrent correlates, antecedents, and type × parenting interactions. *Journal of Adolescence, 25,* 79–92.

Gerris, J. R. M., Houtmans, M. J. M., Kwaaitaal-Roosen, E. M. G., Schipper, J. C., Vermulst, A. A., & Janssens, J. M. A. M. (1998). *Parents, adolescents, and young adults in Dutch families: A longitudinal study.* Nijmegen, The Netherlands: Institute of Family Studies, University of Nijmegen.

Goldberg, L. R. (1992). The development of markers for the big-five factor structure. *Psychological Assessment, 4,* 26–42.

Harrington, D. M., Chin, C. S., Rickey, A. D., & Mohr, J. J. (1999). *Relationships between attachment styles and three increasingly replicable personality types.* Paper presented at the Biennial Meetings of the Society for Research in Child Development, 17 April 1999, Albuquerque, NM, USA.

Hart, D., Hofmann, V., Edelstein, W., & Keller, M. (1997). The relation of childhood personality types to adolescent behaviour and development: A longitudinal study of Icelandic children. *Developmental Psychology, 33,* 195–205.

Haselager, G. J. T., & Van Aken, M. A. G. (1999). *Family and personality, Vol. 1: First measurement wave.* Nijmegen, The Netherlands: University of Nijmegen, Faculty of Social Sciences.

McCrae, R. R., & Costa, P. T. (1994). The stability of personality: Observations and evaluations. *Current Directions in Psychological Science, 3,* 173–175.

Newman, D. L., Caspi, A., Moffitt, T. E., & Silva, P. A. (1997). Antecedents of adult interpersonal functioning: Effects of individual differences in age 3 temperament. *Developmental Psychology, 33*, 206–217.

O'Connor, B. P., & Dvorak, T. (2001). Conditional associations between parental behaviour and adolescent problems: A search for personality-environment interactions. *Journal of Research in Personality, 35*, 1–26.

Roberts, B. W., & DelVecchio, W. F. (2000). The rank-order consistency of personality traits from childhood to old age: A quantitative review of longitudinal studies. *Psychological Bulletin, 126*, 3–25.

Robins, R. W., John, O. P., Caspi, A., Moffitt, T. E., & Stouthamer-Loeber, M. (1996). Resilient, overcontrolled, and undercontrolled boys: Three replicable personality types. *Journal of Personality and Social Psychology, 70*, 157–171.

Scholte, R. H. J., Van Lieshout, C. F. M., & Van Aken, M. A. G. (2001). Relational support in adolescence: Factors, types, and adjustment. *Journal of Research in Adolescence, 11*, 71–94.

Scholte, R. H. J., Van Lieshout, C. F. M., De Wit, C. A. M., & Van Aken, M. A. G. (in press). Adolescent personality types and subtypes and their psychosocial adjustment. *Merril-Palmer Quarterly.*

Van Aken, M. A. G., Van Lieshout, C. F. M., Scholte, R. H. J., & Haselager, G. J. T. (2002). Personality types in childhood and adolescence: Main effects and person–relationship transactions. In L. Pulkkinen & A. Caspi (Eds.), *Pathways to successful development: Personality over the life course.* Cambridge, UK: Cambridge University Press.

EUROPEAN JOURNAL OF DEVELOPMENTAL PSYCHOLOGY, 2004, *1*(4), 349–365

# Family judgements about adolescent problems: Where respondents overlap and why they may disagree

Terry M. Honess

*Department of Psychology, City University, London, UK*

Variation between different family members' appraisals of adolescent adjustment is examined for mothers, fathers and adolescents in 50 families using individual interviews and ratings using the Achenbach check lists. Variation is partly explained by relating these to the concerns each family member expresses about the adolescent's future. Parents appear to operate within a distinct subsystem in talking about concerns and adjustment problems in comparison to their adolescent child. In particular, the parents' concerns about their child's poor attitude appear to drive their assessment of adjustment difficulties; whereas the adolescent appears to be more influenced by concerns about personal relationships outside of the family system. Participants did, however, demonstrate awareness of others' concerns. In social-cognitive terms, appraisals are context sensitive and appear to reflect different criteria for what constitutes social competence.

The influential transactional model of Lazarus and Folkman (1984) defines coping as the cognitive and behavioural management of "specific external and/or internal demands that are appraised as taxing or exceeding the resources of the person" (p. 141). Within the purview of social-cognitive theory, this involves primary appraisal (experience of harm, loss, threat or challenge) and secondary appraisal (what may be done and what are the likely outcomes). These are principal features in the Crick and Dodge (1994) formulation of an information-processing model of social competence.

The aim of this study is to help explain variation between different family members' appraisals of adolescent adjustment by relating these to the concerns each expresses about the adolescent's future. In particular, the contrasting appraisals of parents and their adolescent children are expected to relate to the different preoccupations and concerns which represent the

Correspondence should be addressed to T. M. Honess, Department of Psychology, City University, London, EC1V 0HB, UK. E-mail: T.M.Honess@city.ac.uk

The support of the Economic and Social Research Council (grant no.R000233054) for aspects of this work is gratefully acknowledged.

http://www.tandf.co.uk/journals/pp/17405629.html    DOI: 10.1080/17405620444000229

family's management of rights and responsibilities (Cox & Paley, 1997; Jackson & Rodriguez-Tomé, 1993). In addition, differences between the appraisals of family members may be associated with more specific features of the family system such as the respondent's own mental health and his or her satisfaction with different family relationships. For example, Hay et al. (1999) examined parents' ratings using the Achenbach Child Behaviour Checklist (CBCL) for young children and found moderate convergence between parents ratings. However, mothers' ratings were associated with both her own depression and her view of her marriage, whereas fathers reports were associated with an independent measure of the child's cognitive ability.

Examining older children and adolescents, Mathijssen, Koot, Verhulst, de Bruyn, & Oud (1998) explored the associations of the mother–child, father–child, and mother–father relationship using CBCL ratings of families referred to outpatient mental health services. They found that both the mother–child and the mother–father relationship were related to child problem behaviour. However, whereas the mother–child relationship was more closely related to externalizing behaviour, the mother–father relationship was particularly related to internalizing behaviour. Seiffge-Krenke and Kollmar (1998) also report system effects in that mothers experiencing stress caused by marital problems perceived more problem behaviours in their children, while fathers' perceptions were relatively unaffected by their own personal adjustment.

More generally, agreement on judgements about family members varies with the particular characteristics under question. For example, Branje, van Aken, van Lieshout and Mathijssen (2003) required personality judgements from family members about other family members, including adolescents (aged 11–16 years). Judgements were found to depend on the relevance of personality factors within the family setting: agreeableness and conscientiousness were judged most consistently.

In this study, we focus on the varying views offered by the biological mother and father and their adolescent child in respect of the concerns and problems that may be experienced by the adolescent. Concerns for the coming year are articulated through individual interviews which allow a direct examination of which characteristics are of concern to each respondent. Asking respondents about the future draws on the concept of "future orientation". From this perspective, it is assumed that there is an interdependent relationship between perceived problems and future aspirations and concerns (Nurmi, 1991). In addition to asking each respondent about their concerns for the adolescent in the coming year, each respondent is also asked to anticipate what other family members would say in response to the same question about the adolescent. This allows an examination of other awareness from both parents and the adolescent, for whom there may be new opportunities and demands to "meta-monitor" and revise models of self and parents (Kobak & Cole, 1994).

It is expected that parents will show greater agreement with each other than with their adolescent child for adjustment ratings (e.g., Seiffge-Krenke & Kollmar, 1998) and concerns about the future. This is consistent with the notion of a parent subsystem (Cox & Paley, 1997), notwithstanding the different influences on mother and father ratings discussed above. Convergence of parents' adjustment ratings is, consistent with earlier work (e.g., Hay et al., 1999), expected to be particularly evident for externalizing problems, in contrast to internalizing symptoms. Our novel assessment of participants' concerns about the coming year is expected to shed further light on the reasons why respondents may agree or disagree in their appraisals of the adolescent's adjustment.

## METHOD

*Sample.* The participants were drawn from families with children attending local authority schools in South Glamorgan, Wales and East Sussex, England. The selection of schools allowed a representative range of the families' social background. Parents of children in school years 7 to 9 (ages 12 to 15) were contacted by letter requesting permission for their son or daughter to take part in one of a series of studies concerned with "teenagers and family life". The letters included an invitation for the parents to take part themselves. A reply form and stamped reply envelope was enclosed for return directly to the researchers. The reply form required details of family constitution including number and age of children, the individuals resident in the family home and whether or not there had been a separation or divorce. In total 3% of children were withdrawn by their parents from the planned testing in schools. A high percentage of parents (74%) said they would be willing to take part in a study themselves.

All but two parents from two families agreed to take part in the "interview and questionnaire" project discussed here. For this report, 50 families were involved where there had been no separation, i.e., both biological mother and father were resident. Individual interviews were arranged, in the family home, with the target adolescent and each of his or her parents. In two of the families, work commitments precluded the fathers from taking part in the prearranged interviews. Hence interviews are available from 48 fathers, 50 mothers and 50 adolescents (29 boys and 21 girls, mean age 13.7 years). Each family member was left with a set of questionnaires to be completed and returned by post. A full set of questionnaire answers (i.e., no missing data) were returned by 43 fathers, 45 mothers and 47 adolescents.

*Questionnaires.* This paper reports scores using the Achenbach and McConaughy (1987) scales. Externalizing problems are the sum of the Aggressive and Delinquent Behaviour scales. Internalizing problems are the sum of the Anxious/Depressed, Withdrawn and Attention Problem scales. Finally, the Total problems scores were computed. These are the sum of the two externalizing scales, the three internalizing scales and scales which address Somatic Complaints, Social Withdrawal Problems and Thought Problems.

*Interview schedules.* Following extensive piloting, the final schedule consisted of nine sections and was designed to be used with mothers, fathers and adolescents. The section concerned with anticipated changes over the next year is discussed here. The interviews were tape recorded, transcribed and coded before entry into SPSS. The data were coded, primarily on a question-by-question basis, using a content analysis of verbatim responses to build up category sets. Interrater agreement on the content analysis was shown to be high. Following several reworkings of the original, exploratory category sets, the final coefficients of agreement were based on a fresh sample of twelve interviews (four mothers, two fathers and two adolescents). Adolescent respondents were asked the following questions:

Thinking about the next twelve months

1 What changes, if any, do you see happening in your life over the next year?
2 What changes would you like to see?
3 Are there any things you are concerned or worried about?
4 What changes do you think *your mother* would like to see happening in your life over the next year?
5 Do you think there are any things *she* is concerned or worried about?
6 What changes do you think *your father* would like to see happening in your life over the next year?
7 Do you think there are any things *he* is concerned or worried about?

The format for parents was entirely complementary—e.g., a mother respondent with adolescent son would be asked. "What changes, if any, do you see happening in *your son's* life over the next year?" and so on. The order of mother and father questions was counter-balanced between adolescent respondents.

*Coding of interview responses.*   Table 1 provides a list of the verbatim responses to questions about concern in descending order of frequency of occurrence from all three respondents combined. Table 1 also provides the nine category set (NC to CC) which groups the verbatim responses. The reliability of coding verbatim responses to one of these categories was high, Scott's $\pi = 95\%$ between independent raters.

TABLE 1
Concerns for all respondents

| Summary of verbatim responses[1] | Category[2] |
|---|---|
| 1. General (in sense of common to all adolescents), so not ones that cause fretting or worry | NC |
| 2. Will not do well at school/Concerns over school performance | SP |
| 3. Nothing in particular/Don't know really | NC |
| 4. General attitude problems/not responsible enough. Not motivated/negative attitude/will rebel. Many things of concern. May drop out of society/Slovenly behaviour. | BA |
| 5. Future employment | ED |
| 6. Will not make new friends/friendship problems | PR |
| 7. Will get hurt in boy (girl) friend relationships/unsuitable relationships | PR |
| 8. In danger without adult supervision, especially at night | MC |
| 9. Get in with a bad crowd | PR |
| 10. Health/physical maturation | MH |
| 11. Will choose the wrong career/exam options | ED |
| 12. Education/work transitions | ED |
| 13. Lack of confidence | MC |
| 14. Choice of exams | ED |
| 15. Relationship with sibling | FR |
| 16. School will collapse (financially) | CC |
| 17. Will want to do more things on own/be more independent | MC |
| 18. Won't have a boy/girlfriend | PR |
| 19. Won't mature physically | MH |
| 20. Way adolescent spends money—lack of responsibility | BA |
| 21. Will miss out due to lack of money | CC |
| 22. Will lose principles and beliefs | MC |
| 23. Relationship with parents | FR |
| 24. Won't talk to parents about problems | FR |
| 25. Sibling leaving home so adolescent alone | CC |
| 26. Worries too much, will affect health | MH |
| 27. Moving house so change of school | CC |

[1]The responses are provided in descending order of frequency of occurrence from all three respondents combined.
[2]NC: No particular Concerns. SP: School Progress. BA: Bad Attitude. ED: Educational and work related decisions. PR: Peer Relationships. MC: Maturation–Confidence. MH: Maturation–Health. FR: Family Relationships. CC: Change in Circumstances.

## RESULTS

The data are presented in three sections: first, a description of the concerns articulated by different family members, second, an interrater analysis of the adolescent's current adjustment problems and, third, the relationship between areas of concern and adjustment scores.

### Concerns articulated by different family members

Table 2 provides an overview of the number of individuals who reference a particular category of concern from a particular perspective, i.e., the table shows whether a particular category was mentioned at least once by a respondent. For example, 17 adolescents refer at least once to their own concern over school progress (SP), 15 anticipate that their mother would express such a concern and eight anticipate their father would express such a concern. A total of 26 adolescents report that such a concern would be expressed at least once from their own and/or their parents' perspectives. Individuals frequently reference more than one category of concern. For example, 4 of the 17 adolescents who expressed a concern themselves over SP also expressed a concern over peer relationships (PR). This breakdown is not shown in Table 2. The cumulative impact of concerns is analysed in section 3 of the results.

Adolescents' views indicate SP as the highest area of concern, yet concerns about PR feature highest for both mothers and fathers. With regard to perceptions of other's views, both parents correctly assume their adolescent children will be most concerned about SP. Generally, adolescents predict the pattern for their parents although they underestimate the number of relationship statements that are made by fathers. Notwithstanding this, there is good evidence of the adolescents being sensitive to their parents' different concerns. In particular, maturation (MC and MH) and bad attitude (BA) rarely feature in the adolescents' own concerns (1 person only), yet adolescents do acknowledge that parents may be concerned (11 adolescents for perception of mother's concerns and 12 for perception of father's concerns).

Systematic identification of similarity and difference between respondents' own concerns about the adolescent is restricted by the absolute number of persons reporting concerns. Nonetheless, the observed pattern is consistent with the expectation that parents' concerns show more overlap than that between either parent and the adolescent. Moreover, there is evidence that the different parties (parents and adolescents) are aware of the other's point of view.

TABLE 2

Number of individuals expressing a particular concern about the adolescent from their own view or their perceptions of the views of other family members

*Adolescents (n = 50)*

| Adolescent's view on self | | Perception of mother's view | | Perception of father's view | | From any perspective | |
|---|---|---|---|---|---|---|---|
| SP | 17 | SP | 15 | SP | 8 | SP | 26 |
| PR | 6 | PR | 7 | MC | 6 | PR | 11 |
| ED | 6 | MC | 5 | ED | 4 | ED | 11 |
| FR | 1 | BA | 5 | BA | 4 | MC | 8 |
| MC | 1 | ED | 4 | MH | 2 | BA | 7 |
| CC | 1 | MH | 1 | PR | 1 | FR | 3 |
| MH | — | FR | 1 | FR | 1 | MH | 2 |
| BA | — | CC | — | CC | — | CC | 1 |

*Mothers (n = 50)*

| Mother's view on adolescent | | Perception of adolescent view | | Perception of father's view | | From any perspective | |
|---|---|---|---|---|---|---|---|
| PR | 9 | SP | 11 | SP | 9 | SP | 19 |
| SP | 7 | PR | 5 | ED | 6 | PR | 12 |
| MC | 6 | MH | 3 | PR | 4 | ED | 9 |
| ED | 4 | ED | 2 | BA | 3 | MC | 6 |
| BA | 4 | BA | 1 | MC | 2 | BA | 6 |
| MH | 3 | MC | — | MH | — | MH | 5 |
| FR | 2 | FR | — | FR | — | FR | 2 |
| CC | 2 | CC | — | CC | — | CC | 2 |

*Fathers (n = 48)*

| Father's view on adolescent | | Perception of adolescent view | | Perception of mother's view | | From any perspective | |
|---|---|---|---|---|---|---|---|
| PR | 10 | SP | 10 | SP | 9 | SP | 18 |
| ED | 7 | PR | 5 | BA | 6 | PR | 16 |
| BA | 5 | ED | 4 | PR | 6 | BA | 10 |
| SP | 5 | BA | 3 | MC | 3 | ED | 9 |
| MC | 3 | CC | 2 | ED | 2 | MC | 5 |
| MH | 2 | MH | 1 | MH | — | CC | 3 |
| CC | 1 | MC | — | FR | — | MH | 2 |
| FR | — | FR | — | CC | — | FR | — |

*Note.* See Table 1 for explanation of SP and so on.

## Interrater analysis of the adolescent's current adjustment problems

As outlined in the method section of this report, the Achenbach scales were used: the YSR was completed by adolescents and the CBCL by each parent independently. Table 3 provides descriptive statistics for each rating. It is striking that the adolescent reports substantially more total

TABLE 3
Descriptive statistics by respondent for the total external,
internal and problems
CBCL scores

| Score | M | SD |
|---|---|---|
| TotextF | 6.30 | 6.63 |
| TotextM | 6.58 | 7.27 |
| TotextA | 11.74 | 8.34 |
| TotintF | 4.49 | 4.07 |
| TotintM | 5.56 | 4.42 |
| TotintA | 12.21 | 8.75 |
| TotprobF | 17.53 | 12.99 |
| TotprobM | 18.82 | 14.77 |
| TotprobA | 37.83 | 21.48 |

*Note*: F is the father rating; M the mother; and A the adolescent.

problems, especially internalizing problems compared to his or her parents.

The intrarespondent ratings for internalizing and externalizing problems suggest that these two scales are measuring different aspects of the adolescent's behaviour. For mothers, this was, $r = .53$, $p < .01$, for fathers, $r = .31$, $p < .05$, and for adolescents, $r = .30$, $p < 05$. This is important since they are weaker than the interrater correlations for externalizing problems discussed below (significant for all intra vs. inter comparisons).

Table 4 provides interrater correlations for each rating. There proved to be more than moderate agreement between parents for externalizing problems, $r = .81$, $p < .01$, and total problem scores, $r = .75$, $p < .01$. However, as predicted, this overlap is significantly greater than that shared with their adolescent child (for each of the four parent–adolescent correlation comparisons). Consistent with expectations, overlap between parents for internalizing problems was weak. However, that between father and adolescent was significant, $r = .38$, $p < .05$, though this correlation was not significantly different from that ($r = .22$, NS) between father and mother. Inspection of overlap for the internalizing subscales suggests fathers show more agreement with their adolescents, in comparison to mother's agreement with adolescents, for anxiety and depression, whereas mothers show more agreement, in comparison to father's agreement, for attention problems. However, consistent with expectations of parent agreement with each other for behaviours that are more easily observed, there is close agreement between parents for attention problems, $r = .72$, $p < .01$.

TABLE 4
Interrater analysis of the adolescent's current adjustment problems

| Respondent | Problems | Mother | Adolescent |
|---|---|---|---|
| Father | *Total external* | .81** | .50** |
| Mother | | | .53** |
| Father | Aggression | .76** | .53** |
| Mother | | | .45** |
| Father | Delinquent | .84** | .34* |
| Mother | | | .49** |
| Father | *Total internal* | .22 | .38* |
| Mother | | | .30 |
| Father | Anxiety | .34* | .48** |
| Mother | | | .23 |
| Father | Withdrawal | .31 | .19 |
| Mother | | | .26 |
| Father | Attention | .72** | .19 |
| Mother | | | .35* |
| Father | Somatic problems | .21 | .20 |
| Mother | | | .36* |
| Father | Social problems | .73** | − .01 |
| Mother | | | .08 |
| Father | Thought problems | .13 | .16 |
| Mother | | | .42** |
| Father | *Total problems* | .75** | .38* |
| Mother | | | .34* |

*Note*: Pair-wise deletion was used in computing correlations.
** significant at .01 level (2-tailed); *significant at the .05 level (2-tailed).

In summary, the data are consistent with expectations of agreement in ratings for observable characteristics, especially between mother and father. The findings also allow for the possibility that different respondents may focus on different aspects of the adolescent's behaviour. This possibility is explored in next section.

## Adjustment ratings and their relation to the different concerns about the coming year expressed by each respondent

Concerns expressed in the interview are computed from the total number of references for each category reported by each person. The following variables are considered: NC, SP, BA, ED and PR. Given their low frequency of occurrence, the following categories are not considered independently: CC, FR, MH and MC. In addition, one total concern score is computed, this is a summary of BA, PR, CC, FR, MH and MC. Hence, this score is made up of all categories except those which refer to no concerns (NC) or education concerns only (SP and ED). In the following analysis, respondents' own views and their perceptions of the views of other family members are considered separately. In addition, a composite score of each type of concern was computed for each individual. This is made up of concerns expressed from one's own view and the perception of others' views. The composite score is important since it tracks worries from any perspective and provides variables that better approximate a normal distribution. Table 5 provides descriptive statistics for the composite scores.

The relationship between respondents' concerns and adjustment ratings is provided in Table 6a for mothers, Table 6b for fathers and Table 6c for adolescents. Consider first, a mother's own concerns about her adolescent child (the MM ratings) and her ratings of her child's adjustment. There is a clear pattern in that concerns over her child's poor attitude (MM – BA) relate significantly to all three adjustment ratings, a pattern that is also reflected in the relationships between total concerns score (MM – SUM) and adjustment ratings. The other statistically significant relationship is an understandable inverse relationship between total internalizing problems and reports of no particular concerns about the coming year.

The relationship between the mother's perceptions of the father's concerns (the MF ratings) and her own ratings of her child's adjustment shows a similar pattern to those involving her own concerns, but only reaches statistical significance for the sum of concerns score (MF – SUM) with the total external and total problems ratings. There is a complete absence of overlap between the mother's perceptions of the adolescent's view (the MA set of concerns) and her own adjustment ratings.

Finally, the pattern for mother's own view (the MM concerns) is repeated for the composite concerns scores (the M concerns), which sums concerns

TABLE 5
Descriptive statistics by respondent for all interview-based concerns

| Mother | M | SD | Father | M | SD | Adolescent | M | SD |
|---|---|---|---|---|---|---|---|---|
| Combined[1] | | | Combined | | | Combined | | |
| ED | 0.26 | 0.63 | ED | 0.28 | 0.64 | ED | 0.28 | 0.57 |
| BA | 0.16 | 0.47 | BA | 0.31 | 0.66 | BA | 0.18 | 0.48 |
| NC | 1.18 | 1.0 | NC | 1.06 | 1.0 | NC | 1.42 | 1.0 |
| PR | 0.38 | 0.75 | PR | 0.44 | 0.68 | PR | 0.28 | 0.61 |
| SP | 0.54 | 0.81 | SP | 0.50 | 0.77 | SP | 0.80 | 0.90 |
| SUM[2] | 0.92 | 1.2 | SUM | 1.00 | 1.0 | SUM | 0.84 | 1.2 |

[1]Combined refers to the total number of each set of concerns expressed by each respondent, from his or her own view, combined with his or her perspective on the views of other family members.
[2]The sum of all concerns except those which refer to no concerns or education or school concerns.

TABLE 6(a)
Mothers' adjustment ratings of adolescents and their relation to the different concerns about the coming year expressed by mothers

| N = 45 | Totext | Totint | Tprob |
|---|---|---|---|
| MM-ED[1] | −.05 | −.20 | −.09 |
| MM-BA | .61** | .43** | .58** |
| MM-NC | −.25 | −.30* | −.22 |
| MM-PR | .08 | .09 | .01 |
| MM-SP | .15 | −.07 | .06 |
| MM-SUM[2] | .37* | .38* | .35* |
| MF-ED | −.10 | −.21 | −.17 |
| MF-BA | .21 | .17 | .20 |
| MF-NC | −.20 | −.21 | −.20 |
| MF-PR | .19 | .03 | .08 |
| MF-SP | .08 | −.08 | −.01 |
| MF-SUM | .41** | .29 | .36* |
| MA-ED | .06 | −.24 | .00 |
| MA-BA | −.12 | −.02 | −.13 |
| MA-NC | −.13 | −.15 | −.15 |
| MA-PR | −.08 | −.12 | −.13 |
| MA-SP | .12 | .21 | .19 |
| MA-SUM | −.08 | −.06 | −.12 |
| M-ED[3] | −.05 | −.32* | −.13 |
| M-BA | .43** | .33* | .40** |
| M-NC | −.26 | −.30* | −.26 |
| M-PR | .10 | .03 | −.010 |
| M-SP | .16 | .04 | .12 |
| M-SUM | .37* | .33* | .32* |

[1] MM- the mother's own view, MF mother's perspective on father, MA mother's perspective on adolescent e.g., MM-ED, is mother's own concerns expressed within the Education category.
[2] The sum of all categories except those which refer to no concerns or education or school concerns (see text).
[3] M- refers to the total number of each set of concerns expressed by mother, from her own view and her perspective on the concerns expressed by other family members.

expressed by mother from her own view and her perspectives on the views of the father and the adolescent. That there is a significant inverse relationship between M − ED (the composite score for educational and work-related decisions) and total internalizing problems makes sense in that the mother is reporting issues relating to decisions within the school system, rather than any concerns over her individual child's behaviour.

Turning now to the father's own concerns about his adolescent child (the FF concerns) and his ratings of his or her adjustment (Table 6b), there is a pattern that closely corresponds to the comparable matrix for mothers. Concerns over poor attitude hold particular sway in predicting adjustment ratings. Father's perceptions of the mother's concerns (the FM concerns)

TABLE 6(b)

Fathers' adjustment ratings of adolescents and their relation to the different concerns about the coming year expressed by fathers

| N = 41 | Totext | Totint | Tprob |
|---|---|---|---|
| FF-ED | .01 | −.14 | −.00 |
| FF-BA | .64** | .40** | .64** |
| FF-NC | −.09 | −.23 | −.18 |
| FF-PR | −.08 | .13 | .04 |
| FF-SP | .02 | .08 | −.02 |
| FF-SUM | .32* | .26 | .41** |
| FM-ED | −.05 | −.06 | −.01 |
| FM-BA | .29 | .40** | .36* |
| FM-NC | −.16 | −.44** | −.24 |
| FM-PR | .04 | .23 | .12 |
| FM-SP | .08 | −.08 | .02 |
| FM-SUM | .14 | .52** | .34* |
| FA-ED | .03 | .04 | −.03 |
| FA-BA | −.08 | .36* | −.00 |
| FA-NC | .16 | −.08 | .07 |
| FA-PR | −.07 | .19 | .03 |
| FA-SP | −.06 | .33* | .10 |
| FA-SUM | −.13 | .28 | −.03 |
| F-ED | .01 | −.07 | −.02 |
| F-BA | .53** | .57** | .59** |
| F-NC | −.03 | −.33* | −.16 |
| F-PR | −.06 | .29 | .10 |
| F-SP | .01 | .17 | .06 |
| F-SUM | .23 | .56** | .43** |

*Note.* F is the father rating. See Table 6 (a) footnote for full explanation.

and his own ratings of adjustment problems follow a similar pattern to his own concerns.

There is, however, a contrast between parents: For mothers, perceptions of fathers' concerns relate to her rating of externalizing problems ($r = .41$, $p < .01$) but not internalizing problems ($r = .29$, NS). For fathers, perceptions of mothers' concerns relate to his rating of internalizing problems ($r = .52$, $p < .01$) but not externalizing problems ($r = .14$, NS). In addition, unlike mother respondents, there is some overlap between the father's perceptions of the adolescent's view (the FA−BA and FA−SP concerns) and the father's ratings of internalizing problems. Finally, the pattern for father's own view (the FF concerns) is repeated for the composite score (the F concerns).

Turning now to the adolescent's own concerns for his or her future (the AA concerns, Table 6c), a markedly different pattern is evident. Only two statistically significant relationships emerged: the inverse relation between

TABLE 6(c)
Adolescents' adjustment ratings of self and their relation to the different concerns about
the coming year expressed by adolescents

| N = 47 | Totext | Totint | Tprob |
|---|---|---|---|
| AA-ED | −.04 | .18 | .11 |
| AA-BA | N/a[1] | N/a | N/a |
| AA-NC | .20 | −.35* | −.10 |
| AA-PR | .16 | .22 | .23 |
| AA-SP | −.36* | −.04 | −.26 |
| AA-SUM | .11 | .28 | .24 |
| AM-ED | −.13 | .05 | −.03 |
| AM-BA | .14 | .13 | .15 |
| AM-NC | .08 | −.17 | −.09 |
| AM-PR | .27 | .23 | .32* |
| AM-SP | −.05 | .11 | .04 |
| AM-SUM | .13 | .14 | .17 |
| AF-ED | .04 | −.07 | −.01 |
| AF-BA | −.08 | .45** | .27 |
| AF-NC | .01 | −.13 | −.14 |
| AF-PR | .26 | .05 | .18 |
| AF-SP | .11 | .01 | .09 |
| AF-SUM | .01 | .24 | .21 |
| A-ED | −.06 | .09 | .05 |
| A-BA | .03 | .34* | .25 |
| A-NC | .14 | −.33* | −.16 |
| A-PR | .29* | .26 | .35* |
| A-SP | −.18 | .04 | −.08 |
| A-SUM | .10 | .25 | .25 |

*Note.* A is the father rating. See Table 6 (a) footnote for full explanation.
[1] Not applicable due to absence of adolescent own reports of Bad Attitude.

no concerns and self reports of internalizing problems, and an inverse relation between concerns over school progress and externalizing problems. The adolescent's perceptions of the mother's concerns (the AM concerns) and father's concerns (AF concerns) and his own ratings of adjustment problems reveal just two relationships. First, perceptions of mother's concerns about personal relationships and self-ratings of total problems ($r = .32$, $p < .01$) and, second, perceptions of father's concerns about poor attitudes and self-ratings of internalizing problems ($r = .45$, $p < .01$).

Finally, the relationships between self-ratings of problems and the composite concern scores (the A concerns) is considered. The significant positive relationship between internalizing problems and poor attitude (A−BA) and the inverse relationship with no concerns (A−NC) repeats those evident for mothers and fathers. The relationship between self-reports of both externalizing problems and total problems with the composite score of worries over personal relationships is unique to the adolescent.

## DISCUSSION

The procedure used here allows a direct measure of the extent to which an individual's concerns, as evinced in response to questions about the future, overlap with adjustment ratings. This contrasts with previous work that has examined respondents' adjustment ratings in relation to family process variables, e.g., the quality of different family relationships (e.g., Mathijssen et al., 1998). The current work also adds to earlier research insofar as it examines overlap in adjustment ratings between parents and their adolescent child's own ratings.

Consistent with earlier work, there was convergence of the parents' CBCL ratings for externalizing problems, which also showed significant overlap with the adolescent's own judgements. In contrast, there was relatively little overlap between ratings of internalizing problems. However, there was some evidence of parents showing a different pattern of overlap with their adolescent children—fathers for internalizing anxiety/depression and mothers for attention problems. Indeed, contrary to the findings of Seiffge-Krenke and Kollmar (1998), we did not find that Mothers' ratings, in comparison to fathers', were more closely related to adolescents' self-ratings for either internal or externalizing problems (see Table 4).

A complementary pattern was evident for reports of family members concerns about the coming year for the adolescent. There was clear overlap between parents, but a contrast with the adolescent position. Nonetheless, both parties showed awareness of the other position. This was particularly evident for the adolescents who predicted parents' concerns in respect of maturity (particularly low confidence and poor attitude), without expressing such concerns themselves. Taken together, the concerns expressed by family members support the hypothesis of greater overlap within the parent family subsystem. This is also consistent with the argument that the adolescent is aware of the parental position, but wishes to assert independence and stress difference (Hauser, 1991; Honess et al., 1997).

The relationship between concerns expressed by parents and their adjustment ratings showed substantial overlap, consistent with prediction. In particular, each parent's concerns over their adolescent child's poor attitude was closely related to not only externalizing problems, as might be expected, but also to internalizing problems. This finding is a not a simple function of intrarater correspondence reflecting "mother's view of the child" and "father's view of the child" (cf. Hay et al., 1999) since agreement between parents for externalizing problems was greater than parent intrarater agreement on internalizing and externalizing problems. No other category of concerns showed such clear overlap, except an understandable inverse relationship between lack of concerns and ratings of adjustment problems.

Each parent's anticipation of the other parent's concerns showed a similar pattern of relationships with adjustment ratings. The notable exception was that mother's perception of father's concerns related to her rating of externalizing problems but not internalizing problems. For fathers, perceptions of mothers' concerns related to his rating of internalizing problems but not externalizing problems. It may be speculated that each parent is reflecting the common social script that mothers know more about thoughts and feelings (internalizing problems); whereas fathers know more about the adolescents' behaviour (externalizing problems).

Perhaps surprisingly, a mother's anticipation of the concerns expressed by the adolescent showed no relationship with her adjustment ratings; whereas there was some evidence that a father's anticipation of the adolescent's concerns did relate to his own adjustment ratings. It is plausible that a parent, in this case the father, might expect their view of the adolescent's adjustment to be reflected in the concerns the adolescent expresses. If this is the case, it is difficult to explain why this didn't also operate for the mother. Adolescents, as expected, showed no similarity with parents in respect of relations between expressed concerns and adjustment ratings. For example (see Table 6c), adolescents showed significant relations between their own ratings of externalizing problems and total problems with the composite score of concerns over personal relationships, a pattern that was absent for parents.

In summary, it has been demonstrated that parents appear to operate within a distinct subsystem in talking about concerns and adjustment problems in comparison to their adolescent child. In particular, the parents' concerns about their children's poor attitude appear to drive their assessment of adjustment difficulties; whereas the adolescent appears to be more influenced by concerns about personal relationships outside of the family system. In social-cognitive terms, appraisals of threat and concern are context sensitive and appear to reflect different criteria for what constitutes "social competence" (Crick & Dodge, 1994), insofar as adolescents are clearly aware of their parents' position.

There are, however, some distinct differences between parents: fathers alone appear to relate their adjustment worries to their perception of the adolescent's views. In addition, fathers relate their perception of mothers' concerns about the adolescent to their own ratings of internalizing problems; whereas mothers relate fathers concerns to externalizing problems. It is only for adolescents that the composite score seems particularly important, researchers would be advised to solicit an adolescent's view of what his mother and father might say in order to explore more fully the preoccupations that affect an adolescent's adjustment ratings.

In conclusion, it is argued that a direct examination of the concerns of family members does aid the explanation of why family members may disagree on adjustment ratings. However, the direction of influence between concern and adjustment and that between parents and the adolescent (see Cook, 2001; Kerr & Stattin, 2003) should be explored in a longitudinal design. This is particularly important since such change is constrained by broader, often contested, norms (Bosma, Jackson, Zijsling, Zani, Charman, & Honess, 1996; Margolin, Blyth, & Carbone, 1988; Matsueda, 1992). Finally, sample size should allow exploration of the effect of the four different parent–adolescent gender dyads (Russell & Saebel, 1997) in order to provide more evidence-based interpretations of mother and father differences in adjustment ratings.

# REFERENCES

Achenbach, T. M., & McConaughy, S. H. (1987). *Empirically based assessment of child and adolescent psychopathology: Practical applications.* Thousand Oaks, CA: Sage.

Bosma, H. A., Jackson, S., Zijsling, D. H., Zani, B., Charman, E. A., & Honess, T. M. (1996). Who has the final say? Decisions on adolescent behaviour within the family. *Journal of Adolescence, 19*(3), 277–291.

Branje, S. J. T., van Aken, M. A. G., van Lieshout, C. F. M., & Mathijssen, J. J. P. (2003). Personality judgments in adolescents' families: The perceiver, the target, their relationship, and the family. *Journal of Personality, 71*(1), 49–81.

Cook, W. L. (2001). Interpersonal influence in family systems: A social relations model analysis. *Child Development, 72*(4), 1179–1197.

Cox, M. J., & Paley, B. (1997). Families as systems. *Annual Review of Psychology, 48*, 243–267.

Crick, N., & Dodge, K. A. (1994). A review and reformulation of social information-processing mechanisms in children's social adjustment. *Psychological Bulletin, 115*(1), 74–101.

Hauser, S. T. (1991). *Adolescents and their families.* New York: Free Press.

Hay, D. F., Pawlby, S., Sharp, D., Schmuecker, G., Mills, A., Allen, H., & Kumar, R. (1999). Parents' judgements about young children's problems: Why mothers and fathers might disagree yet still predict later outcomes. *Journal of Child Psychology & Psychiatry & Allied Disciplines, 40*(8), 1249–1258.

Honess, T. M., Charman, E. A., Zani, B., Cicognani, E., Xerri, M. L., Jackson, A. E., & Bosma, H. A. (1997). Conflict between parents and adolescents: Variation as a function of family constitution. *British Journal of Developmental Psychology, 15*(3), 367–385.

Jackson, S., & Rodriguez-Tomé, H. (Eds.). (1993). *Adolescence and its social worlds.* Hove, UK: Lawrence Erlbaum Associates Ltd.

Kerr, M., & Stattin, H. (2003). Parenting of adolescents: Action or reaction? In A. Crouter & A. Booth (Eds.), *Children's influence on family dynamics: The neglected side of family relationships* (pp. 121–151). Mahwah, NJ: Lawrence Erlbaum Associates, Inc.

Kobak, R., & Cole, H. (1994). Attachment and meta-monitoring: Implications for adolescent autonomy and psychopathology. In D. Cicchetti & S. L. Toth (Eds.), *Disorders and dysfunctions of the self. Rochester Symposium on Developmental Psychopathology* (Vol. 5, pp. 267–297). Rochester, NY: University of Rochester Press.

Lazarus, R. S., & Folkman, S. (1984). *Stress, appraisal and coping*. New York: Springer-Verlag.

Margolin, L., Blyth, D., & Carbone, D. (1988). The family as a looking glass: Interpreting family influences on adolescent self-esteem from a symbolic interaction perspective. *Journal of Early Adolescence, 8*(3), 211–224.

Mathijssen, J. J. P., Koot, H. M., Verhulst, F. C., De Bruyn, E. J., & Oud, J. H. L. (1998). The relationship between mutual family relations and child psychopathology. *Journal of Child Psychology & Psychiatry & Allied Disciplines, 39*(4), 477–487.

Matsueda, R. L. (1992). Reflected appraisals, parental labeling, and delinquency: Specifying a symbolic interactionist theory. *American Journal of Sociology, 97*(6), 1577–1611.

Nurmi, J.-E. (1991). How do adolescents see their future? A review of the development of future orientation and planning. *Developmental Review, 11*(1), 1–59.

Russell, A., & Saebel, J. (1997). Mother–son, mother–daughter, father–son, and father–daughter: Are they distinct relationships? *Developmental Review, 17*(2), 111–147.

Seiffge-Krenke, I., & Kollmar, F. (1998). Discrepancies between mothers' and fathers' perceptions of sons' and daughters' problem behaviour: A longitudinal analysis of parent–adolescent agreement on internalising and externalising problem behaviour. *Journal of Child Psychology & Psychiatry & Allied Disciplines, 39*(5), 687–697.

EUROPEAN JOURNAL OF DEVELOPMENTAL PSYCHOLOGY, 2004, *1*(4), 367–382

# Adaptive and maladaptive coping styles: Does intervention change anything?

Inge Seiffge-Krenke

*Johannes Gutenberg-Universität Mainz, Germany*

Research on adolescent development has devoted little attention to the social and cognitive processes that are linked to adaptive or maladaptive psychological outcomes. This is surprising, since it is widely acknowledged that most adolescents are confronted with a wide range of normative and non-normative stressors, which may tax their emotional and cognitive resources (Compas, Hinden, & Gerhardt, 1995). Because increased psychosocial stress during this developmental period is a significant and pervasive risk factor for psychopathology (Compas, Connor-Smith, Saltzman, Thomsen, & Wadsworth, 2001), the ways in which adolescents cope with these stressors are potentially important mediators and moderators of the impact of stress on current and future adjustment. In this regard it is important to note that although a substantial number of adolescents meet the criteria for emotional or behavioural psychopathology, they rarely take up offers of professional help (Zwaanswijk, van der Emde, Verhaak, Bensing, & Verhulst, 2003). Yet, it is not fully known how social cognitive factors are related to this pattern of use of mental health services by adolescents.

This contribution focuses on the coping behaviours of adolescents who have adaptive and maladaptive outcomes. More specifically, it deals with coping as a core process, which is linked to current and future social functioning in adolescents. In addition, it tries to illustrate how social cognitive processes may contribute to the "counselling aversion" (Seiffge-Krenke, 1998) seen in emotionally troubled adolescents.

## COPING AND SOCIAL COGNITIVE DEVELOPMENT

The most prominent and frequently occurring stressors during adolescence are related to issues of self-image, physical changes associated with pubertal development, peer and family conflicts, academic problems, school

Address correspondence to Inge Seiffge-Krenke, Psychologisches Institut der Johannes Gutenberg-Universität Mainz, Staudinger Weg 9, 55099 Mainz, Germany.
E-mail: seiffge@uni-mainz.de

http://www.tandf.co.uk/journals/pp/17405629.html    DOI: 10.1080/17405620444000247

transitions, and initiating and maintaining romantic relationships (Bagley & Mallick, 1995; Nieder & Seiffge-Krenke, 2001; Pollina & Snell, 1999; Seiffge-Krenke, Weidemann, Fentner, Aegenheister, & Poeblau, 2001; Smetana, Yau, & Hanson, 1991). As these stressors emerge, adolescents are still developing the capacity to regulate their emotions (Seiffge-Krenke, 2002). In this regard, they may be increasingly challenged to reflect about their actions and the consequences thereof. For example, when coping with problems at school or in the family, adolescents may become intensely concerned about which actions are the "right" ones in terms of how others will react (Seiffge-Krenke et al., 2001). Indeed, we may consider coping as an excellent example of what social cognitive development in adolescence is all about.

Eighty-two percent of the everyday stressors adolescents must cope with are associated with issues involving social relationships, e.g., quarrels with parents, arguments with teachers, and various conflicts in close relationships with friends and romantic partners (Seiffge-Krenke, 1995). It is interesting that although much stress occurs as a result of negative social interaction, most coping processes occur in the context of social relationships. For example, adolescents generally prefer to deal with these relationship stressors by talking about the conflict with the person concerned and/or seeking support from parents and friends (Ebata & Moos, 1995; Frydenberg, 1997; Seiffge-Krenke, 1995; Stark, Spirito, Williams, & Gueremont, 1989). However, research findings suggest that adolescents make strong cognitive efforts in coping with relationship stressors. In this regard it is noteworthy that cognitive processes play a key role in early conceptualizations of coping put forth by Lazarus and Folkman (1991), who described coping as a process of continuous cognitive appraisals and reappraisals of the stressful encounter.

Studies using a variety of research methods have generated data that show that adolescents are continuously confronted with relationship stressors, and that cognitions in solving these problems and conflicts are significantly important (Seiffge-Krenke, 1995; Seiffge-Krenke et al., 2001). In particular, two different research methods were employed in order to assess coping with relationship stressors. Anticipatory coping in response to eight age-typical stressors was assessed by the Coping Across Situations Questionnaire (CASQ; Seiffge-Krenke, 1995), which has been employed by many different investigators around the world (Gelhaar et al., 2004). Cross-cultural studies have basically confirmed the existence of two adaptive, functional coping styles: (1) "active coping" which encompasses the coping strategy of active support seeking; and (2) "internal coping", which refers to the strategy of reflecting about the problem. Another coping style, termed "withdrawal", was also identified. Adolescents who exhibit this style of coping avoid the stressor, thereby leaving the problem unresolved. As will be discussed below, although this coping style may be a meaningful way of dealing with certain stressors, in the long run, it can be also considered as maladaptive. In addition, the Coping Process Interview (Seiffge-Krenke, 1995; Seiffge-Krenke et al., 2001) was used to examine coping immediately after a stressful event had taken place. Based on Lazarus and Folkman's (1991) model of coping, primary appraisal (e.g., perceived stressfulness), secondary appraisal (e.g., identification of the availability of own resources or social support for coping with the stressor), and tertiary appraisal (e.g., evaluation of the effects of coping) were explored.

## The role of cognition in adaptive coping styles

Research on coping using the CASQ has been conducted on over 9000 adolescents, aged 12 to 20 years, in 22 countries in Europe, Africa, Asia, and North America. In all of the samples investigated, adolescents employed the two adaptive modes of coping (i.e., active support seeking and internal reflection on possible solutions) most frequently, whereas withdrawal was used to a lesser extent (Seiffge-Krenke, 1993; Seiffge-Krenke, 1995; Gelhaar et al., 2004).

As indicated in Figure 1, roughly equal proportions adolescents used active coping (38%) and internal coping (39%) to deal with stressors, and 23% showed withdrawal from the stressful situation. Some cross-cultural differences are worth noting. For example, adolescents from Finland and the Czech Republic had the highest rates in internal coping, i.e., they preferred to reflect about possible solutions to a problem (Gelhaar et al., 2004).

The information obtained during the Coping Process Interview with adolescents immediately after the stressor had taken place revealed that reflection was much greater than had been assessed for anticipatory coping

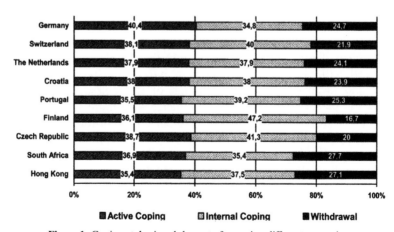

**Figure 1.** Coping styles in adolescents from nine different countries.

using the CASQ (Seiffge-Krenke et al., 2001). Stressors associated with relationship issues elicited the highest rates of reflection about possible solutions. Compared to the CASQ findings, information obtained from the Coping Process Interviews showed that active coping was not very prominent immediately after the stressor had occurred. Instead, the most frequent imminent coping response could be characterized as a blockade of action. According to the information obtained in the Coping Process Interviews, cognitive processes accounted for a considerable proportion of coping responses overall.

In summary, two basic coping styles are most prominent when adolescents deal with age-typical stressors. Active support seeking, i.e., turning to the concerned person or soliciting assistance from the social network, especially peers and friends, is a common mode of coping with relationships stressors. In addition, adolescents typically deal with relationship stressors at a cognitive level, i.e., they reflect a great deal about possible solutions for solving conflicts in relationships.

## Age differences in coping: A sign of further social cognitive development

Although developmental changes in response to relationship stressors might be expected, this has not been thoroughly investigated. This is, in part, due to the use of inappropriate sampling procedures, whereby adolescents are often lumped together in samples that may include children or adults. (Compas et al., 2001; Patterson & McCubbin, 1987). Nieder and Seiffge-Krenke (2001) observed that after the age of 15, adolescents tried more frequently to obtain support from peers and friends when they had problems in romantic relationships, and that they increasingly discussed their conflicts with people who were in a similar situation. More important, they were more likely to address the individual with whom they had had a conflict and attempt to discuss or resolve the problem, while keeping their emotions under control. These age-related changes in the use of social support were intertwined with developmental changes marked by increased cognitive abilities and social maturity. After the age of 15, adolescents increasingly adopted the perspective of significant others, were more willing to make compromises or yield to the wishes of others. In addition, they reflected more about possible solutions to their problems, thus cultivating a variety of coping options (Seiffge-Krenke, 1995). All in all, significant changes in 10 of the 20 coping strategies in the CASQ were found to be related to age (Seiffge-Krenke, 1995). These changes in the style of coping with relationship stressors pertained equally to active support seeking as well as to reflection about possible solutions to problems. These findings on social cognitive development thus support and elaborate upon those reported by other investigators who have shown that the abilities to anticipate and acknowledge the perspective of others (Case, Hayward, Lewis, & Hurst, 1988), employ metacognitive strategies, and reflect on emotions (Steinberg, 1993) increase throughout the adolescent years.

The impact of social-cognitive maturity on coping also becomes obvious when comparing factor structures in different age samples. Kavšek and Seiffge-Krenke (1996) found that after the age of 15, approach-oriented coping could be split up into behavioural and cognitive components, whereas avoidance remained the same from 11 to 19 years. A recent study using growth-curve modelling (Seiffge-Krenke & Beyers, 2004) has substantiated these findings by showing that cognitive processes in coping are relevant from early adolescence onwards and become even more important as adolescents grow older. In diverse samples, internal coping increased from 21 to 53% between the ages of 14 and 21 years.

## DEVELOPMENTAL FACTORS CONTRIBUTING TO A MALADAPTIVE OUTCOME

Compas, Hinden, and Gerhardt (1995) have described different trajectories for adolescent development. One subgroup of adolescents shows stable, adaptive functioning; another subgroup shows stable yet maladaptive functioning. Stable adaptive functioning is typically seen in adolescents who traverse adolescence in relatively low-risk environments. Stable, maladaptive functioning is characteristic for the developmental trajectories of individuals who enter adolescence with a history of problems or psychosocial disorders and who are exposed to chronic stress and adversity in the absence of social or personal resources that mitigate against these risks. Research has identified avoidant coping as a risk factor for this maladaptive outcome (Seiffge-Krenke, 1998). Here, avoidant coping encompasses the cognitive coping response of trying not to think about the problem as well as more maladaptive strategies, e.g., dealing with negative emotions by withdrawing or trying to forget the problem by consuming alcohol or drugs.

### Avoidant coping: A common coping style in clinical samples

Maladaptive coping styles are very prominent in clinically referred samples of adolescents. In one study, the rates of withdrawal for a sample of 46 adolescents receiving psychiatric care were nearly two-times higher than those in the healthy control group of 289 adolescents and amounted to over 40% of the coping responses for some stressors (Seiffge-Krenke, 1998). In another sample of 120 adolescents seeking help at a counselling centre, a substantial association between behavioural and emotional problems and avoidant coping was found (Seiffge-Krenke, 1998). The correlations between the Youth Self-Report (YSR) Total Score and withdrawal amounted to $r = .52$, $p < .001$ for females and $r = .42$, $p = .05$ for males. A solid link between avoidant coping and increased symptomatology has also been established in longitudinal studies (Herman-Stahl, Stemmler, & Petersen, 1995; Seiffge-Krenke, 2000; Seiffge-Krenke & Klessinger, 2000). In all of these studies it was shown that approach-oriented copers reported the lowest number of symptoms of depression, whereas avoidant copers reported the highest.

## Are avoidant coping and withdrawal always maladaptive?

For over 25 years, there has been much debate about which coping strategies are adaptive and which are not (Compas et al., 2001; Lazarus, 1998; Patterson & McCubbin, 1987). However, in recent years our understanding of defence mechanisms has changed, and hence, there appears to be more consensus about this issue. Contributions from the fields of cognitive and developmental psychology have encouraged some investigators to suggest that defences such as avoidance can be seen as alternative adaptive strategies when people must deal with major stressors (Cramer, 2000). Thus, avoidance may be associated with a positive outcome in the short term, particularly in case of highly stressful, unalterable events such as severe illness (Kazak & Meadows, 1989). However, the positive effects of using avoidant coping may wane with time. The findings on clinically disturbed adolescents presented above clearly illustrate this. For example, irrespective of the problem at hand, the majority of these adolescents rather uniformly used withdrawal as a predominant coping style. It is possible that these adolescents lacked the ability to discriminate adequately between types of stressors and characteristics of stressful events. In the long run, the weakness of this cognitive function could lead to maladaptive functioning. The capacity to adopt a flexible coping style according to the demands of various stressful situations is thus a prerequisite of adaptive coping. Taken together, although avoidant coping and withdrawal are meaningful ways of dealing with stressors the adolescent perceives as uncontrollable, the cross-situational use of this coping style over a longer time period is clearly maladaptive.

## Is there no return from a maladaptive pathway?

There is, unfortunately, little evidence to encourage hopes that an adolescent may be able to depart from a maladaptive pathway. The subjects in

Herman-Stahl et al.'s (1995) study, who switched from avoidant (e.g., withdrawal) to approach coping (e.g., active coping and internal coping) during one year, displayed a significant decrease in depression. Conversely, those who changed from approach to avoidant coping showed a significant increase in depressive symptoms. Furthermore, it has been shown that all types of avoidant coping, whether stable or not, are linked to serious symptomatology, e.g., depression, even two years later (Seiffge-Krenke & Klessinger, 2000).

Further research using longitudinal samples is needed to clarify the links between maladaptive coping and externalizing syndromes such as aggression and antisocial behaviour. There is some evidence that delinquent adolescents not only show elevated withdrawal rates but also less internal coping, compared to non-conspicuous controls (Lösel, Bliesener, & Köferl, 1989). This may suggest a deficit in the capacity for reflection about possible solutions, a finding which is important in designing intervention strategies. In a study on antisocial adolescents, Seiffge-Krenke (1998) found that these deficits, once established, remained rather stable or even increased. Figure 2 illustrates, based on the CASQ, that although there were small increases in adaptive coping styles in antisocial adolescents, their progression was negligible compared to same-aged controls. Antisocial adolescents also showed higher levels of external emotional regulation, e.g., letting out anger by shouting or slamming doors, and they showed an increased tendency to forget their problems by consuming drugs and alcohol.

## The impact of working models of attachment

Coping with age-typical stressors in adolescence builds on earlier experiences. A growing body of work suggests that attachment theory (Bowlby, 1969, 1988) is a useful framework for explaining why individuals differ in the ways that they deal with stressors and for understanding how these differences develop from childhood to adulthood. Bowlby argued that through repeated experiences with attachment figures, children develop mental representations, or internal working models, of themselves and others. These working models centre on the availability and responsiveness of others, and the worthiness of the self. Once developed, these working models will be activated and used to guide behaviour in times of stress. A central notion of attachment theory is that individuals retain their early working models of self and others into adulthood, and that these models are used to predict and manage stressful encounters, especially in relationships with significant others.

These conceptualizations of internal working models parallel Lazarus and Folkman's (1991) model of coping, according to which individual

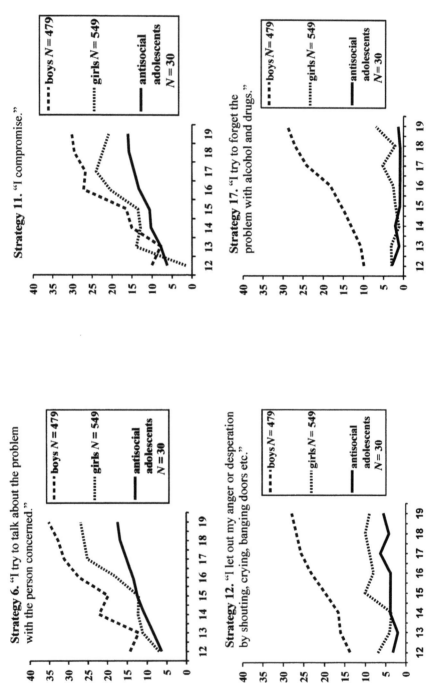

**Figure 2.** Differences in coping strategies in normal and antisocial adolescents.

differences are believed to mediate the appraisal process. This mediation has a bearing on the subsequent selection and use of coping strategies, which, in turn, determines how adaptive an outcome will be. Internal working models could be influential in the perception of stress during the primary appraisal process and, in particular, guide the individual during the secondary appraisal, when requesting and receiving support are crucial. From a developmental perspective it is important to note that it has been repeatedly demonstrated that different working models are linked to different reactions to stress in infancy and childhood (Anders & Tucker, 2000; Urban, Carlson, Egeland, & Sroufe, 1991). These working models remain valid in adolescence (Allen, Moore, Kuperminc, & Bell, 1998) and become relatively stable aspects of personality (Shaver, Belsky, & Brennan, 2000). Seiffge-Krenke and Beyers (2004) found that adolescents classified as having secure internal working models dealt with their problems more actively by using their social network during adolescence and the transitions to young adulthood. In contrast, individuals with dismissed internal working models used less support seeking and more internal coping than those with preoccupied working models. Latent growth curve modelling revealed that between 14 and 21 years of age, the rates of change in the use of active and internal coping differed between individuals with secure and insecure working models, whereby the rates for both coping styles among participants in the secure group increased more dramatically than for those in the insecure group. Only minor differences were found with respect to withdrawal as a coping style.

Some studies have further elucidated the links between family climate and coping styles. Adolescents stemming from cohesive, expressive, and individuated families report comparably low levels of stress and exhibit the highest level of active coping and the lowest levels of withdrawal or avoidant coping (Seiffge-Krenke, 1995). In contrast, adolescents who come from disengaged and conflict-oriented families report a great many relationship stressors in diverse areas (such as parent–adolescent relationships, friendships, and romantic relationships) and exhibit a low level of active coping and a high level of withdrawal. Taken together, these findings highlight the positive contributions that a supportive and enriching family environment make towards an adolescent's development of adaptive coping styles.

## Deficits in social support and network structure of distressed adolescents

In trying to explain the high stability of maladaptive coping styles, it is important to acknowledge research findings that concern the pitfalls of social-support network structures and obstacles in using social support.

Lazarus (1985) was one of the first who argued that close relationships may not necessarily represent the optimal social support structure, warning that sayings such as "a friend is the best medicine" trivialize the multiple and often contradictory functions of social support.

In exploring the relation between social skills and healthy social functioning, Johnson (1991) showed that individuals who exhibited psychopathological symptomatology were less likely to initiate or maintain positive social relationships than individuals who showed no symptoms. Moreover, Cotterell (1994) found that distressed adolescents had distorted views of how social networks function. Compared to asymptomatic adolescents, those with psychopathological symptomatology reported a significantly greater portion of their social network relationships as being very close and cited a larger number of members in their networks who provided them with much support. Yet, during the interviews, the distressed adolescents reported that although their "friends" had provided them with high levels of support in times of stress, the relationships dissolved a few days later.

When they are troubled or have problems, adolescents may turn to peers because they believe that they will be able to provide emotional support (Hartup & Stevens, 1997). However, some evidence has been obtained to indicate that peer-oriented social activities may be associated with poorer health outcome and increased problem behaviour. For example, Arnett (1990) showed that much of adolescents' impulsive, risk-taking behaviour occurred in the context of their social activities with peers, either as a central goal of their interaction or as an outgrowth of initially more benign activities. In general, research on resiliency has demonstrated that the ability to solicit alternative social support from others is very crucial. In a study of adolescents whose parents had major affective disturbances, Beardslee and Podorefsky (1988) found that half of the adolescents who showed positive adaptation reported having turned to someone outside the immediate family during episodes of acute parental illness, including adults. Thus, it appears that distressed adolescents may benefit from increasing and deepening their associations with supportive adult figures.

## Lack of social support, maladaptive coping and symptomatology: A vicious circle

Most individuals pass through adolescence without developing major psychological problems (Compas et al., 1995). However, adolescents with stable yet maladaptive outcomes show specific characteristics (Seiffge-Krenke, 1998). First, most of them have experienced an accumulation of major stressors. Second, as the number of stressors increases, the predominantly active coping style of most adolescents begins to adopt features of avoidance or withdrawal. Thus, a lack of discriminatory power and a rather inflexible application of a certain coping mode are characteristic for this group. Third, in some subgroups of adolescents showing maladaptive outcomes, for example, antisocial and delinquent adolescents, deficits in cognitive dimensions of coping emerge. Fourth, deficits in social support and network structure contribute to maladaptive functioning. As detailed above, a lack of social support and severe disruption in close relationships were characteristic of most adolescents in clinical samples. It would be adaptive for the adolescent who experiences negative family relationships to be able to compensate for the lack of support in the family by turning to friends, other relatives, or unrelated adults. However, the specific attachment history of these adolescents may persist in other relationship patterns, e.g., if the adolescent achieves low support in his or her immediate family, the likelihood that support will be sought outside of the immediate family is also low (Cassidy & Shaver, 1999). The accumulation of stressors, a dysfunctional coping style, and deficits in relationships create a vicious circle, thus contributing to increased symptomatology. It is clear that adolescents in clinical samples find it extremely difficult to consider or apply compensatory processes, especially if this vicious circle has existed for some time (East & Rook, 1992; Saunders, Resnick, Hoberman, & Blum, 1994). In this regard, these findings have clear implications for prevention and intervention.

## DOES INTERVENTION CHANGE ANYTHING?

Although many adolescents show psychopathological symptoms, the majority are disinclined to seek professional counselling. Only about 20 to 30% of adolescents in various European countries who claim they have problems actually seek professional help (Saunders et al., 1994; Sourander, Helstelä, Ristkari, Ikeheimao, Helenius, & Piha, 2001). As will be discussed further below, intervention in troubled adolescents seems to be as effective as for patients of other ages. There remains, however, the challenge of motivating adolescent to begin therapy.

### Effectiveness of intervention programs

If the question of effectiveness of intervention programs for adolescents is approached in a conventional way, i.e., by comparing it with the effectiveness of intervention programs based on parent–adult interactions and counselling, it is safe to say that treatment of adolescents is effective. Nevertheless, it must be acknowledged that more adolescents are less motivated to participate in therapy than adults are, and that more adolescents drop out from therapy programs than adults do. In their *meta-analyses* of studies on adolescent samples, Gomes-Schwartz (1978) and Tramontana (1980) reported that psychotherapy showed positive effects in 75% of the adolescents studied. This percentage was only slightly below that for adult patients and above the 39% spontaneous remission rate for adolescents. Weisz, Weiss, Alicke, and Klotz (1987) addressed the question of treatment effectiveness in their meta-analysis of 108 well-designed outcome studies of 4- to 18-year-old patients. Across various outcome measures, the average child or adolescent who underwent therapy was better adjusted than 79% of those who received no therapy. Therapy proved to be more effective for children (mean effect size of .92) than for adolescents (mean effect size of .58). In any case, these studies suggest that when adolescents agree to undergo treatment for problems, they can profit considerably. Indeed, other more-recent studies converge in showing that treatment of adolescents is effective (Hibbs, 2001; Kazdin, Bass, Ayres, & Rodgers, 1990).

It is important to note that the efficacy rates for therapeutic treatment differed depending on symptoms. The meta-analyses converge in showing that efficacy rates were lower for externalizing symptoms, including antisocial, aggressive behaviours, than for internalizing symptoms like depression. However, adolescents who agreed to undergo therapy developed more positive attitudes about the benefits of accepting help when they were troubled. Based on information elicited in interviews conducted with 46 adolescents who were just beginning therapy and again after approximately six months of treatment, Seiffge-Krenke (1998) found that the percentage of adolescents who expressed ambivalence or negative motivation decreased from 67 to 35%. At the same time, fears and doubts about the efficacy of therapy were diminished. In the first few weeks, 42% of the adolescents expressed such reservations; after six months of treatment, only 5% reported such thoughts. This may be due to the fact that within this time, 57% of the patients showed clear improvements in their symptoms. In the interviews, the majority of adolescents described therapy or counselling as a difficult but worthwhile process. This indicates that positive experiences during the course of treatment had a favourable effect on their attitudes.

In this study, it was important that the adolescent patients considered the counsellor or therapist as someone they could trust and with whom they might discuss anything that worried them. To a certain extent the therapist was seen as a model of constructive coping behaviour. Although the adolescent's relationship with the therapist was overshadowed by mistrust, fear, and uncertainty at the beginning of treatment, a working alliance was eventually established, and the adolescent began to focus on achieving his or her therapeutic goals. Thus, even adolescents with an initially ambivalent or rejecting attitude toward emotional health care may be able to change their negative expectations and redefine their hopes for improvement. In any case, the study showed that when adolescents do agree to take part in intervention programs or undergo individual treatment, they can profit enormously from the experience.

## Is peer group counselling a promising alternative?

Based on the discussion above, it is easy to understand why attempts to provide intervention may fail. In searching for alternatives, peer support group counselling may not only be more economical but also more effective in helping adolescents in distress before more serious problems develop. The peer support approach may also encourage adolescents to assume an active role in dealing with their problems. Due to the more egalitarian structure of communication between peers, highly stressed adolescents may be more likely to feel at ease about talking about their problems in the peer setting.

Some research findings suggest that peer counselling is quite effective. However, based on Dishion, McCord and Poulin's (1999) overview of this topic, caution is warranted. These authors studied the subtle but powerful influence of deviant friendships on escalation in problem behaviour during adolescence and also tested the hypothesis that high-risk youth potentially escalate their problem behaviour in the context of interventions delivered by youth. They found, for example, that the intervention approach using peer support groups for adolescents with antisocial problems appeared to contribute to an increase in these adolescents' risk behaviours. The Cambridge-Sommerville Youth Study examined crime prevention in delinquent youths, based on the knowledge that high-risk adolescents lack affectionate guidance. The research group conducting the study selected normal and antisocial boys for treatment including summer camps. The risk ratio for a bad outcome was 1:10, and it even increased when the antisocial boys attended the summer camp twice. They found that boys with the poorest relationships and the most delinquency were most vulnerable to the negative effects of peer-group counselling, or "deviancy training" (as the investigators termed it) with respect to increasing delinquent behaviour. Thus, repetition of contact within the peer-group intervention created an iatrogenic effect, which was confirmed in further experimental studies.

Lipsley (1992) analysed hundreds of controlled intervention studies, which focused on adolescent problem behaviour, and found that about 29% of peer counselling approaches in juvenile delinquent treatment showed negative effects. This is probably an underestimate, since researchers are disinclined to report no, or negative, effects. Therefore, intervention approaches based on bringing many adolescents with antisocial behaviour problems together may unwittingly produce increases in problem behaviour.

This is not restricted to antisocial behaviour, since similar effects have been found with respect to depression. For example, peer support was found to be correlated with an increase in physical complaints and depression in adolescent females (Seiffge-Krenke, 1998).

Although these findings may cast some doubt on the efficacy of using peer counselling to help troubled adolescents, there are some more positive findings. In his overview of positive youth development, Reed Larson (2000) found convincing evidence to show that participation in certain youth activities involving peers (e.g., sports, music groups, or special-interest organizations) was instrumental for promoting the development of initiative and responsibility. Although this may not seem surprising, the findings do help to point out how important it may be to choose the proper kind of peer context for helping troubled adolescents.

## REFERENCES

Allen, J. P., Moore, V. M., Kuperminc, G. P., & Bell, K. L. (1998). Attachment and adolescent psychosocial functioning. *Child Development, 69,* 1406–1419.

Anders, S. L., & Tucker, J. S. (2000). Adult attachment style, interpersonal competence, and social support. *Personal Relationships, 7,* 379–389.

Arnett, J. (1990). Contraceptive use, sensation seeking and adolescent egocentrism. *Personality and Individual Differences, 11,* 541–546.

Bagley, C., & Mallick, K. (1995). Negative self-perception and components of stress in Canadian, British, and Hong Kong adolescents. *Perceptual and Motor Skills, 81,* 123–127.

Beardslee, W. R., & Podorefsky, D. (1988). Resilient adolescents whose parents have serious affective and other psychiatric disorders: Importance of self-understanding and relationships. *American Journal of Psychiatry, 145,* 63–69.

Bowlby, J. (1969). *Attachment and loss, Vol. 1. Attachment.* New York: Basic Books.

Bowlby, J. (1988). *A secure base: Clinical applications of attachment theory.* London: Routledge.

Case, R., Hayward, S., Lewis, M. D., & Hurst, P. (1988). Toward a neo-Piagetian theory of cognitive and emotional development. *Developmental Review, 8,* 1–51.

Cassidy, J., & Shaver, P. R. (Eds.). (1999). *Handbook of attachment: Theory, research, and clinical applications.* New York: The Guilford Press.

Compas, B. E., Connor-Smith, J. K., Saltzman, H., Thomsen, A. H., & Wadsworth, M. (2001). Coping with stress during childhood and adolescence: Progress, problems, and potential. *Psychological Bulletin, 127,* 87–127.

Compas, B. E., Hinden, B. R., & Gerhardt, C. A. (1995). Adolescent development: Pathways and processes of risk and resilience. *Annual Review of Psychology, 46,* 265–293.

Cotterell, J. L. (1994). Analyzing the strength of supportive ties in adolescent social supports. In F. Nestmann & K. Hurrelmann (Eds.). *Social networks and social support in childhood and adolescence* (pp. 257–267). New York: de Gruyter.

Cramer, P. (2000). Defense mechanisms in psychology today. Further processes for adaptation. *American Psychologist, 55,* 637–646.

Dishion, T. J., McCord, J., & Poulin, F. (1999). When interventions harm: Peer groups and problem behavior. *American Psychologist, 54,* 755–764.

East, P. L., & Rook, K. S. (1992). Compensatory patterns of support among children's peer relationships: A test using school friends, nonschool friends, and siblings. *Developmental Psychology, 28,* 163–172.

Ebata, A. T., & Moos, R. H. (1994). Personal, situational and contextual correlates of coping in adolescence. *Journal of Research in Adolescence, 4*, 99–125.

Frydenberg, E. (1997). *Stress and coping*. London: Routledge.

Gelhaar, T., Seiffge-Krenke, I., Bosma, H., Cunha, M., Gillespie, C., Lam, R., Loncaric, D., Macek, P., Steinhausen, H.-C., Tam, V., & Winkler-Metzge, C. (2004). An international perspective on coping behavior in adolescence. *Manuscript submitted for publication.*

Gomes-Schwartz, B. (1978). Effective ingredients in psychotherapy: Prediction of outcome from process variables. *Journal of Consulting and Clinical Psychology, 46*, 1023–1035.

Hartup, W. W., & Stevens, N. (1997). Friendships and adaptation in the life course. *Psychological Bulletin, 121*, 355–370.

Herman-Stahl, M. A., Stemmler, M., & Petersen, A. C. (1995). Approach and avoidant coping: Implications for adolescents' mental health. *Journal of Youth and Adolescence, 24*, 649–655.

Hibbs, E. D. (2001). Evaluating empirically based psychotherapy research for children and adolescents. *European Child and Adolescent Psychiatry, 10*, 3–11.

Johnson, T. P. (1991). Mental health, social relations, and social selection: A longitudinal analysis. *Journal of Health and Social Behavior, 32*, 408–423.

Kavšek, M., & Seiffge-Krenke, I. (1996). The differentiation of coping traits in adolescence. *International Journal of Behavioral Development, 19*, 651–668.

Kazak, A. E., & Meadows, A. T. (1989). Families of young adolescents who had survived cancer: Social-emotional adjustment, adaptability, and social support. *Journal of Pediatric Psychology, 14*, 175–192.

Kazdin, P. C., Bass, D., Ayres, W. A., & Rodgers, A. (1990). Empirical and clinical focus of child and adolescent psychotherapy research. *Journal of Consulting and Clinical Psychology, 58*, 366–380.

Larson, R. (2000). Towards a psychology of positive youth development. *American Psychologist, 55*, 170–183.

Lazarus, R. S. (1985). The trivialization of distress. In P. Ahmed & N. Ahmed (Eds.), *Coping with juvenile diabetes* (pp. 33–60). Springfield, IL: Charles C. Thomas.

Lazarus, R. S. (1998). *Fifty years of the research and theory of R. S. Lazarus*. Mahwah, NJ: Lawrence Erlbaum Associates, Inc.

Lazarus, R. S., & Folkman, S. (1991). *Stress, appraisal, and coping* (3rd ed.). New York: Springer.

Lipsey, M. W. (1992). Juvenile delinquency treatment: A meta-analytic inquiry into the variability of effects. In T. D. Cook, H. Cooper, D. S. Cordray, H. Hartmann, L. V. Hedges, R. J. Light, T. A. Louis, & F. Mosteller (Eds.), *Meta-analysis for explanation: A casebook*. New York: Russell Sage Foundation.

Lösel, F., Bliesener, T., & Köferl, P. (1989). On the concept of "unvulnerability". Evaluation and first results of the Bielefeld Project. In M. Bambring, F. Lösel, & H. Skowronek (Eds.), *Children at risk: Assessment, longitudinal research, and intervention* (pp. 186–221). New York: de Gruyter.

Nieder, T., & Seiffge-Krenke, I. (2001). Coping with stress in different phases of romantic development. *Journal of Adolescence, 24*, 297–311.

Patterson, J. M., & McCubbin, H. J. (1987). Adolescent coping style and behaviors: Conceptualization and measurement. *Journal of Adolescence, 10*, 163–186.

Pollina, L. K., & Snell, W. E., Jr. (1999). Coping in intimate relationships: Development of the Multidimensional Intimate Coping Questionnaire. *Journal of Social and Personal Relationships, 16*, 133–144.

Poulin, F., Dishion, T. J., & Haas, E. (1999). The peer influence paradox: Friendship quality and deviancy training within male adolescent friendships. *Merrill-Palmer Quarterly, 45*, 42–61.

Saunders, S., Resnick, M., Hoberman, H., & Blum, R. (1994). Formal help-seeking behavior of adolescents identifying themselves as having mental health problems. *Journal of the American Academy of Child and Adolescent Psychiatry, 33,* 718–728.

Seiffge-Krenke, I. (1993). Coping behavior in normal and clinical samples: More similarities than differences? *Journal of Adolescence, 16,* 285–304.

Seiffge-Krenke, I. (1995). *Stress, coping, and relationships in adolescence.* Mahwah, NJ: Lawrence Erlbaum Associates, Inc.

Seiffge-Krenke, I. (1998). *Adolescents' health: A developmental perspective.* Mahwah, NJ: Lawrence Erlbaum Associates, Inc.

Seiffge-Krenke, I. (2000). Causal links between stressful events, coping style, and adolescent symptomatology. *Journal of Adolescence, 23,* 675–691.

Seiffge-Krenke, I. (2001). *Diabetic adolescents and their families: Stress, coping, and adaptation.* New York: Cambridge University Press.

Seiffge-Krenke, I. (2002). Emotionale Kompetenz im Jugendalter: Ressourcen und Gefährdungen [Emotional competence in adolescence: Resources and potential dangers]. In M. v. Salisch (Ed.), *Emotionale Kompetenz entwickeln. Grundlagen in Kindheit und Jugend* [Developing emotional competence. Foundations in childhood and adolescence] (pp. 51–72). Stuttgart: Kohlhammer.

Seiffge-Krenke, I., & Beyers, W. (2004). The impact of internal working models of attachment on coping styles. *Manuscript submitted for publication.*

Seiffge-Krenke, I., & Klessinger, N. (2000). Long-term effects of avoidant coping on adolescents' depressive symptoms. *Journal of Youth and Adolescence, 29,* 617–630.

Seiffge-Krenke, I., Weidemann, S., Fentner, S., Aegenheister, N., & Poeblau, M. (2001). Coping with school-related stress and family stress in healthy and clinically referred adolescents. *European Psychologist, 6*(2), 123–132.

Shaver, P. P., Belsky, J., & Brennan, K. (2000). The adult attachment interview and self-reports of romantic attachment: Associations across domains and methods. *Personal Relationships, 7,* 25–43.

Smetana, J. G., Yau, J., & Hanson, S. (1991). Conflict resolution in families with adolescents. *Journal of Research on Adolescence, 1,* 189–206.

Soraunder, A., Helstelä, I., Ristkari, T., Ikeheimao, K., Helenius, H., & Piha, J. (2001). Child and adolescent mental health service use in Finland. *Social Psychiatry and Psychiatric Epidemiology, 36,* 294–298.

Stark, L. J., Spirito, A., Williams, C. A., & Guevremont, D. C. (1989). Common problems and coping strategies I: Findings with normal adolescents. *Journal of Abnormal Child Psychology, 17,* 203–212.

Steinberg, L. D. (1993). *Adolescence.* New York: Knopf.

Tramontana, M. G. (1980). Critical review of research on psychotherapy outcome with adolescents. *Psychological Bulletin, 88,* 429–450.

Urban, J., Carlson, E., Egeland, B., & Sroufe, L. (1991). Patterns of individual adaptation across childhood. *Development and Psychopathology, 3,* 445–560.

Weisz, J. R., Weiss, B., Alicke, M. D., & Klotz, M. L. (1987). Effectiveness of psychotherapy with children and adolescents: Meta-analytic findings for clinicians. *Journal of Consulting and Clinical Psychology, 55,* 542–549.

Zwaanswijk, M., van der Emde, J., Verhaak, P. E. M., Bensing, J. M., & Verhulst, F. C. (2003). Factors associated with adolescent mental health service need and utilization. *Journal of the American Academy of Child and Adolescent Psychiatry, 42,* 1–9.

EUROPEAN JOURNAL OF DEVELOPMENTAL PSYCHOLOGY, 2004, *1*(4), 383–397

# Does intervention change anything? New directions in promoting positive youth development

William M. Kurtines, Marilyn J. Montgomery,
Lisa Lewis Arango and Gabrielle A. Kortsch
*Department of Psychology, Florida International University, USA*

Although a literature on interventions that promote positive development has begun to emerge, important gaps concerning these interventions continue to exist. As part of our program of research, we have made an effort to begin addressing these gaps. An overview of a research project conducted using two sets of multi-ethnic data drawn from the Miami Youth Development Project (Kurtines, Montgomery, Lewis Arango, & Kortsch, 2001) is presented. Though tentative and preliminary, the findings from the project provide preliminary evidence for the success of Changing Lives Program (CLP) in promoting positive qualitative change. Specifically, the results document a relation between participation in CLP and short-term qualitative longitudinal change in life course experiences at the individual developmental level. The basic pattern of qualitative change for participants in the CLP intervention condition tended to be positive, significant, and in the hypothesized direction relative to non-intervention controls, suggesting that intervention does effect positive change.

The literature on promoting positive youth development emerged out of the recognition that interventions targeting troubled (multi-problem) youth need to do more than "treat" problem behaviours (i.e., symptoms) or "prevent" negative developmental outcomes (Lerner, Fisher, & Weinberg, 2000). Recent reviews of programs that promote positive youth development (for example, Catalano, Berglund, Ryan, Lonczak, & Hawkins' 1999 review

Correspondence should be addressed to William M. Kurtines, Department of Psychology, Florida International University, Miami, FL 33199, USA. E-mail: kurtines@fiu.edu

This paper describes the work of the Youth Development Project of the Child and Family Psychosocial Research Center, Department of Psychology, Florida International University, Miami, Florida, 33199.

Thanks to (in alphabetical order): Richard Albrecht, Donette Archer, Ondina Arrufat, Marlene Arzola, Alan M. Berman, Steven L. Berman, Ervin Briones, Janene Bussell, Carolyn Cass Lorente, Laura Ferrer-Wreder, Arlen Garcia, Clary Milnitsky, Seth Schwartz, Silvia Sullivan, Sara K. Swenson

http://www.tandf.co.uk/journals/pp/17405629.html      DOI: 10.1080/17405620444000210

of 25 well-evaluated programs) reveal an accumulation of evidence that the programs do have an impact on young people and that studies of these programs made considerable strides, including increased methodological rigour and sophistication. The answer to the question posed by the title of this paper is thus *yes*, but it is a qualified yes.

## NEW PROBLEMS AND NEW POPULATIONS: PROMOTING POSITIVE YOUTH DEVELOPMENT

Despite the consistent pattern of overall positive findings in the literature, important gaps in research-based knowledge with respect to the impact of youth development interventions still exist. The Catalano review, for example, reported only relatively short-term (pre, post, + follow-ups) studies with outcomes evaluated in terms of magnitude of short-term quantitative change in continuous variables relative to a comparison or control condition. Indeed, consistent with criteria common to the intervention field, this was a core component of the definition of "well-evaluated."

The emphasis on short-term outcome studies using quantitative measures and variable-oriented data analytic strategies that characterizes the literature on treatment, prevention, and positive development intervention programs is useful in many ways. However, it places methodological limits on the types of questions that we can ask and the types of answers that we can obtain, particularly in evaluating positive development programs that target troubled youth. We use the term "troubled" youth to describe the population we work with (and develop interventions for) rather than "behaviour problem," "at-risk," or "normative" youth because although the youth we work with come to our programs with problem behaviours (indeed, typically with multiple problems) and/or are at risk for multiple negative developmental outcomes, our intervention is not designed to target specific behaviour problems, risk factors, or positive domains. Thus, our programs differ from treatment and prevention programs in that although our programs provide (as needed and available) selected interventions that target specific behaviour problems and risk/protective factors (e.g., substance use/abuse, risky sexual behaviours, etc.), reducing behaviour problems and modifying risk/protective factors is not our main goal. Moreover, our programs differ from universal youth development programs in the USA, such as the Boy/Girl Scouts, 4H, etc., which aim at facilitating development along a developmental trajectory or life course that is already proceeding in a positive direction. In contrast to such universal youth development programs, our programs target troubled (multi-problem youth) in community settings and aim at altering or changing the course of lives that are proceeding in a negative direction.

Employed as a selective intervention, the aim of our program is to alter or change the "negative" direction of the life course or pathway of the youth in our programs. That is, we aim to change the lives of troubled young people for the better, where "change" means a qualitative change in direction and where "for the better" is understood as positive in ways that are contextually situated (e.g., relative to each individual's specific life course trajectory at the time of entry into the program) as well as culturally, historically, and developmentally appropriate. Our goal is thus to promote positive qualitative change in participants' lives in ways that are individually, culturally, historically, and developmentally meaningful and significant. We consequently consider our programs to be open-ended responses that target the intersection of the developmental and historical moment—changing lives in changing times (Lerner et al., 2000).

## THE MIAMI YOUTH DEVELOPMENT PROJECT (YDP): THE CHANGING LIVES PROGRAM (CLP)

The *Changing Lives Program* (CLP) is one of the programs currently being developed as part of the *Miami Youth Development Project* (YDP; http:// w3.fiu.edu/ydp/). The YDP is the result of efforts to create a university-community collaboration based on research-related principles consistent with the outreach research model, i.e., a model that focuses on generating innovative knowledge of effective intervention strategies that is also palatable, feasible, durable, affordable, and sustainable in "real-world" settings (Jensen, Hoagwood, & Trickett, 1999; Lerner et al., 2000). The CLP is school-based counselling intervention that uses a participatory learning and transformative approach to create contexts in which troubled (multi-problem) young people can change their lives for the better by taking responsibility for their lives and their communities.

The CLP, now in its second decade of existence, began as a grass-roots response to an urgent and growing need in the community—the need of young people to find themselves and to be reconnected with their lives and families. It has subsequently evolved into a broad-based community partnership. The partnership now consists of *Florida International University* (FIU) (http://www.fiu.edu/choice.html), the public research university in Miami; *Communities in Schools* (CIS) (http://www.cisnet.org/), a private, non-profit organization that is part of a community-based national network for delivering community resources to schools; and *Miami-Dade County Public Schools* (MDCPS) (http://www.dadeschools.net/), the fourth largest school system in the United States, with community-based alternative public high schools located throughout greater Miami. CLP counselling services provided by the YDP are currently available to all of the MDCPS alternative high schools, serving approximately 200 to 250 students each year. A multi-ethnic population of youth come to the alternative schools with a history of attendance, behaviour, or motivational problems in their neighbourhood school, and many come from inner city, low-income families who live in disempowering community contexts of pervasive violence, crime, substance abuse, and limited access to resources.

## NEW THEORIES AND METHODS: THE CHALLENGE OF EXPANDING HORIZONS

Since the mid-twentieth century, the scientific study of human developmental change has been undergoing a dramatic shift in orientation at all levels. During this period, theoretical approaches to understanding developmental change underwent dramatic change, shifting away from conceptualizing developmental change as general, universal, and unidirectional to a focus on the organism's plasticity, from a holistic or person-cantered perspective, and with a view of development as selective age-graded change in adaptive capacity across the life span, from conception to old age.

### Theoretical challenges

In this context, as our theoretical framework evolved, the CLP drew its developmental framework (i.e., theory of what changes and how it changes) from both psychosocial developmental theory (Erikson, 1968) and life course theory (Elder, 1998). Thus, we refer to our framework as a "psychosocial developmental life course" approach. From psychosocial developmental theory, this approach adopts a view of adolescence as the developmental stage at which the individual is first confronted with the difficult challenge (and responsibility) of choosing the goals, roles, and beliefs that give life direction and purpose as well as coherence and integration (i.e., a positive sense of identity). From life course theory, it adopts an emphasis on how individuals construct their own life course through the choices and actions they make within the constraints and opportunities of history and social circumstances. For its intervention strategies (i.e., theory of what to change and how to change it), YDP draws its theoretical framework from Freire's (1970/1983) transformative pedagogy (a pedagogy of dialogue rather than instruction) for empowering marginalized people by enhancing critical consciousness.

### Methodological challenges

In our role as practitioners and educators, we work with young people who come to us in need of change. They find their lives moving in directions that they do not necessarily want them to move in, and in desperate need of help to turn their lives around. As practitioners and educators, we work to create contexts in which they can find themselves and reconnect with their lives and families. Our goal is to help them transform the negative direction of their lives—to get them launched in positive directions—and we often have the sense that we succeed. As researchers, however, we find it difficult to fully document our successes. The measures that we use in investigating our programs capture increases in indices of positive development and decreases in behaviour problems and risk factors, and the data analytic strategies we use to assess the statistical significance of this quantitative change, but providing evidence for the type of qualitative life change that is at the heart of our efforts has proved to be a challenge. Therefore, we added another, related agenda to our program of research: to contribute to advancing the methods that are available for studying developmental change by refining measures for assessing qualitative life course change.

## MEASURING QUALITATIVE LIFE COURSE CHANGE

With the goal of program evaluation, we made a systematic effort to document qualitative life course change in our school based intervention in terms of the expressed meaning and significance of the life course experiences of participants in the intervention. This has involved the adoption, adaptation, and refinement of the two qualitative performance measures of self-development (both designed for indexing the expressed meaning and significance of participants life course experiences) for use in the YDP:

- The Life Course Interview (LCI) (Clausen, 1998) is an individually administered open-ended unstructured "full" response qualitative performance measure of self-development intended for use in conducting comprehensive qualitative analysis (with relatively small samples) focusing on the meaning and significance of participants' experiences of identity transformations across the life course; and
- The *Possible Selves Questionnaire – Qualitative Extension* (PSQ-QE), a qualitative extension of the Possible Selves Questionnaire (PSQ; Oyserman, 1987) refined for use as a group (or individually) administered open-ended "brief" response qualitative performance measure of self development. The PSQ-QE is intended for use in conducting qualitative analysis (with large samples) focusing on the meaning and significance participants' possible future selves.

In addition, we have also developed a framework for the use of relational data analysis in evaluating the CLP. This framework, *Relational Data Analysis* (RDA), evolved out of efforts to develop a practical, ready-at-hand methodological framework for moderating the methodological splits (e.g., subject – object, quantitative – qualitative, interpretation – observation, variation – transformation, nature – nurture, etc.) that have characterized developmental science (Overton, 2003). Specifically, our goal was to draw on well-established qualitative and quantitative research methods and procedures, and on relational metatheory (Overton, 1998, 2003) and its embodied person-centred approach to unifying the strengths of both qualitative and quantitative research traditions.

## WHAT HAVE WE LEARNED? WHERE DO WE GO FROM HERE?

We conducted an RDA of qualitative change in life course experiences using two sets of multi-ethnic data drawn from the Miami YDP (Kurtines et al., 2001). The results of this study illustrate what we have learned so far and suggest future directions for research.

### Relational data analysis: Life Course Interview

The outcome measure used for the RDA of the first set of data for the Kurtines et al. (2001) study was the *Life Course Interview* (LCI). The adaptation of the LCI that we use for the Miami YDP builds on Clausen's (1998) pioneering work on the use of life reviews and life stories in life course research. The LCI is administered twice a year, once at the beginning of the fall semester as part of a pre-evaluation battery and once again at the end of the spring semester as part of the end-of-year evaluation. The data set consisted of 32 participants—22 high school adolescents who participated in the CLP and 10 control students at the same high school. For the LCI data, the audiotaped interviews yielded a total of 448 codable transcriptions records (TRs). From these, response data from 64 Personal Identity and 64 Undergoing Turning Point TRs were analyzed using RDA.

The conceptual and theoretical coding phases of RDA for the *Personal Identity* TRs yielded four theoretically meaningful categories (Negative Identity, Diffused – Uncertain, Confused – Moratorium, Self-assured/Secure Identity) and associated subcategories with a moderately complex structure (see Figure 1a), providing evidence for the utility of RDA as a method for identifying theoretically meaningful categories in open-ended and unstructured interview response data.

The findings also provided clear evidence for the concurrent and construct validity of the LCI when analyzed using RDA. The Conceptual and Theoretical Analysis phases of RDA were designed to be conducted by two independent sets of coders representative of two levels of "theoretical saturation," *theory neutral* (i.e., *not* representative of any particular theoretical perspective) and *theory laden* (i.e., representative of the theoretical coders' consensual understanding of the particular theoretical perspective that they exemplify). An analysis of the exact match of the

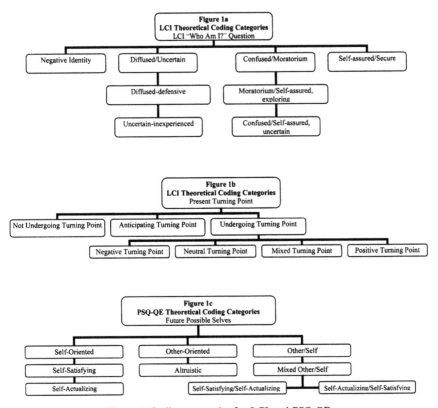

**Figure 1.** Coding categories for LCI and PSQ-QE.

category classifications by the two sets of independent coders (i.e., the conceptual and theoretical coders) for this data set yielded 100% agreement for the Negative Identity category, 85.4% for Diffused–Uncertain, 85.3% Confused–Moratorium, and 81.6% Self-assured/Secure Identity. The overall agreement across all categories was 88.1%, providing strong evidence for concurrence across types of coders.

Because the data were collected using a mixed (within and between) quasi-experimental comparison control design, it was also possible to evaluate the strength of the association between participation in the CLP intervention condition and qualitative changes in the hypothesized direction of positive development using variable-oriented quantitative data analytic strategies. Because the research hypothesis investigated focused on both between and within group differences (assessments repeated over time), the variable-oriented data analytic procedure selected for use was a mixed design Repeated Measures Multivariate Analysis of Variance (RMANOVA), with

Personal Identity as the dependent variable. An RMANOVA was used to evaluate the magnitude of the association between intervention participation (yes – no) and qualitative change in identity category classification over time (same – different), with and without tests for potential moderating effects of gender and/or ethnicity. The results indicated no significant main effect for the repeated factor time but a highly significant time × condition interaction in the hypothesized direction and no significant interaction trend for time × gender and time × ethnicity. Thus, although there were some differential patterns, the basic pattern of qualitative change for participants in the CLP intervention condition tended to be positive, significant, and in the hypothesized direction relative to non-intervention controls.

The conceptual and theoretical coding phases for *Present Turning Point* resulted in the identification of three theoretical categories (Not Undergoing Turning Point, Anticipating Turning Point, and Undergoing Turning Point) and four subcategories (Negative, Neutral, Mixed, Positive Turning Point) also with a moderately complex structure (see Figure 1b). In addition, an exact match analysis again also provided evidence for the construct validity of the LCI yielding for this data set the following average percent agreement: 93.6% Not Undergoing Turning Point category; 78.8% Anticipating Turning Point; 87.5% Undergoing Negative Turning Point; 87.5% Undergoing Neutral Turning Point; 93.8% Undergoing Mixed Turning Point; and 90% for the Undergoing Positive Turning Point category. The overall agreement across all categories and subcategories was 88.4%, again providing strong evidence for concurrence across types of coders.

Finally, the LTP RMANOVAs yielded a significant time × condition interaction in the hypothesized direction with participants in the CLP intervention condition reporting that they anticipated or were undergoing a positive life turning point significantly more often than participants in the control condition. In addition, the results showed no other 2-, 3-, or 4-way interactions, indicating that these results were not significantly moderated by gender or ethnicity.

## Relational data analysis: Possible selves questionnaire – qualitative extension

The outcome measure used for the RDA of the second set of data was the PSQ-QE, which builds on the PSQ (Oyserman, 1987). The PSQ-QE is an extension of the PSQ, adapted and refined for use in our program research to provide a method for eliciting the expressed meaning and significance of participants' possible future selves that could be used as a qualitative measure of a core component of self-development. The data set consisted of 96 participants (73 intervention, 23 controls). Of the 96 in intervention, 43 completed a PSQ-QE as part of CLP's core assessment battery during their pre (fall) evaluation, a mid-year (winter) evaluation, and a year-end (spring) evaluation. The RDA analysis included 175 TRs. The findings of the RDA analysis of the PSQ-QE data, like the LCI analysis, provided evidence for the methodological and theoretical utility of the PSQ-QE as an open-ended (unstructured) "brief" response qualitative index of a core component of self-development, only in this case with a measure that can be group administered to relatively large samples.

The conceptual and theoretical coding phases of RDA yielded three theoretical categories (Self-oriented, Other-oriented, Other/Self) and six associated subcategories (Self-satisfying, Self-actualizing, Altruistic, Mixed Other/Self, Self-satisfying/Self-actualizing, Self-actualizing/Self-satisfying) of future possible selves, again providing evidence for the utility of RDA as a method for identifying theoretically meaningful categories in open-ended and unstructured interview response data. The organizational structure of the categories and subcategories was moderately complex (see Figure 1c).

An exact match analysis provided evidence for the construct validity of the PSQ-QE, yielding the following average percent agreement: 95.4% Self-oriented, Self-satisfying category; 87.5% Self-oriented, Self-actualizing; 92.5% Other-oriented, Altruistic; 85.6% Other/Self, Self-satisfying/Self-actualizing; and 84.4% Other/Self, and Self-actualizing/Self-satisfying. The overall average percent agreement across all categories and subcategories was 89.1%

## PSQ-QE positive intervention gains: Pre – post change (intervention versus control)

Because the PSQ-QE is a "brief" response qualitative index and can, consequently, feasibly be group administered to relatively a large sample across multiple conditions (intervention, control) and across multiple assessment periods (fall, mid-year, year-end), it was possible with this data set to investigate not only participant intervention gains (pre to mid-year) relative to the control condition, but also intervention maintenance (pre, mid-year, year-end) for participants in the CLP intervention condition. In addition, the additional data points also made it possible to explore more fully the complex moderating effects of gender and ethnicity on CLP intervention response in this richly multicultural/multi-ethnic population of adolescents.

An RMANOVA that used PSQ-QE as a dependent variable to evaluate positive intervention gains pre to post yielded a significant time effect, no significant time $\times$ condition interaction, and a highly significant time $\times$ condition $\times$ gender interaction effect ($p < .001$).

From Figure 2 it can be seen that for the participants in the CLP intervention condition, the basic pattern of intervention gain for the PSQ-QE paralleled that of the LCI, i.e., the directionality of the basic pattern of change was positive with qualitative change for participants of both genders and all three ethnic groups tending to change in a positive direction, in this case, from Self-satisfying to Self-actualizing/Self-satisfying, relative to the control condition. As can also be seen from Figure 2, the directionality of the basic pattern of change in the control condition from pre to mid-year was negative, with the direction of qualitative change trending from Self-actualizing/Self-satisfying to Self-satisfying. Of additional significance from a diversity perspective, however, this basic pattern varied across gender or ethnicity, with participants of both genders and the three ethnic groups displaying differential patterns of change over the semester. For example, the females in the control condition moved in a positive direction (similar to the CLP intervention condition) while males in the control condition moved in a negative direction over the semester. The pattern of change in the control condition also showed a similar pattern of moderated change across ethnic groups. White non-Hispanics and Black/African Americans in the control condition tended to move in a negative direction over the semester while Latin/Hispanic participants tended to move in a positive direction.

## Maintenance of intervention gains

A second RMANOVA was conducted using the 43 participants in the CLP condition to determine whether the intervention gains from pre to mid-year were maintained at year-end and to explore whether the maintenance of intervention gains was moderated by gender and ethnicity. Because the analysis of intervention maintenance involved evaluating patterns of change over more than two time points (i.e., pre, mid-year, year-end), tests of within-subject contrasts for the repeated factor time and time × gender and ethnicity interaction effects were conducted for PSQ-QE. The use of tests of within-subject contrasts allowed for modelling patterns of individual change over time (e.g., within-group change assessed at multiple times). In modelling change, within-subject contrasts for the repeated factor evaluate the curvilinear as well as the linear component of change (i.e., quadratic), allowing for a more complex and complete examination of potential moderators of outcome differences. The tests of within-subject contrasts for the repeated factor time and time × gender and ethnicity interaction effects indicated that the trends for the direction of qualitative change as assessed by PSQ-QE were: (1) positive from pre to mid-year and maintained at the year-end evaluation; and (2) significantly moderated by gender and ethnicity. An examination of the tests of within-subject contrasts further indicated that while the time × gender and the time × ethnicity interactions

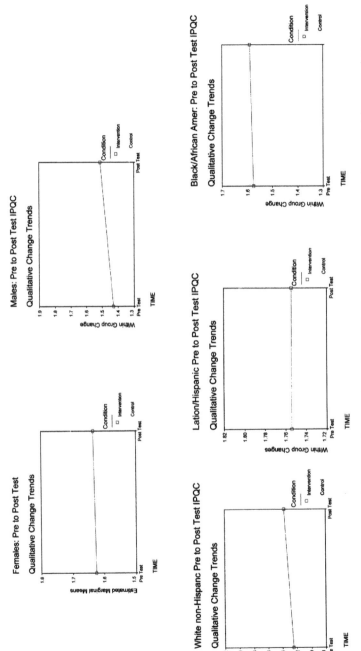

**Figure 2.** OPQC profile plots of significant four-way interaction effects for time × condition × gender × ethnicity: pre and post.

were not significant, there was a significant linear component for the time ×
gender × ethnicity interaction effect in the hypothesized positive direction.
More significant, the quadratic component was *not* significant indicating
that there was no significant change in the year-end evaluation from the
positive direction of the pre to mid-year change, i.e., that the positive
directional change was maintained at year-end evaluation.

An examination of the multivariate tests of significance for the between-
group effects revealed the same pattern of change as for the within-group
contrasts. Specifically, although the main effect for the repeated factor time
was significant, the time × gender and the time × ethnicity interaction were
not significant, there was a significant time × gender × ethnicity interaction
effect. Figure 3 presents the profile plots of significant interaction effects for
the intervention condition for the three assessment times: pre, mid-year,
year-end. From the top left profile plot in Figure 3 it can be seen that for the
intervention condition, the positive directionality of the basic pattern of
change from post to year-end was maintained. As the figure shows, although
the basic trends did not increase from mid-year to year-end, they also did
not decrease, i.e., the gains were maintained.

What the remainder of the profile plots show (and the significant time ×
gender × ethnicity interaction effect supports), however, was that this
overall pattern was significantly moderated by gender and ethnicity. The
main source of the moderation effects of pre to post change was from the
differences in the pattern of change by gender and ethnicity. Figure 3 further
illustrates the complex nature of this interaction. The top centre profile plot,
for example, shows both females and males gain over time and maintain
their gains. It also shows, however, that males tended to begin the
intervention groups characterizing their future possible selves as Self-
satisfying at pre and to undergo greater change in the direction of
characterizing their future possible selves as realizing potentials (Self-
actualizing) and/or benefits to others (Altruistic) at post.

The top-right profile plot, the time × ethnicity interaction, similarly
shows that all three ethnic groups gain over time and maintain their gains. It
also shows, however, that Latino/Hispanic participants tended to begin the
intervention least likely to be characterized as Self-satisfying and they were
also least likely to make gains over time and that White non-Hispanics
tended to begin the intervention most likely to be characterized as Self-
satisfying and were most likely to make gains over time.

Finally, Figure 3 further shows how the pattern of change described by
the two-way time × gender and time × ethnicity interactions were further
qualified by the significant three-way time × gender × ethnicity interaction
effect. The findings represented by these profile plots are also highly
suggestive with respect to the issue of amenability to treatment, which
concerns the identification of subgroups of individuals who are likely to be

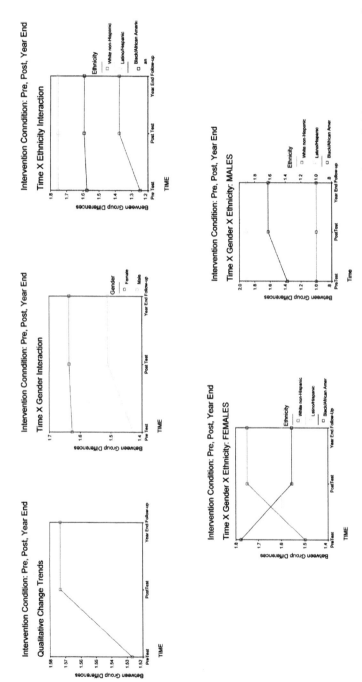

**Figure 3.** OPQC profile plots of significant interaction effects for the three-way interaction effects for time × gender × ethnicity: pre, post, year-end, follow up.

395

the most amenable or responsive to a treatment, an issue that has recently come to the foreground in the literature on the development of interventions that target young people.

## DISCUSSION

We began by noting that the answer to the question posed by the title of this paper, "Does intervention change anything?" is yes, but we can now add that it is a multiply qualified yes. Young people in our intervention did change in ways that we think are positive, and RDA appears to make an important potential contribution as a data analytic framework that can detect such change (and with the potential for unifying the long-standing methodological split that has characterized the study of human development).

One result of the traditional focus on short-term variational (quantitative) change rather than transformational (qualitative) change is that our knowledge about how interventions are related to the reduction of risky or problem behaviours far outstrips our knowledge of how they are related to the qualitative change in the life course prospects of the individual. That is, little is known about whether such interventions increase the likelihood of qualitative change in the life course experiences, and even less is known about the types of intervention strategies that might facilitate qualitative life course change. As part of our program of research, we consider our work on CLP a contribution to the evolution of positive youth development programs that target changing the lives in troubled youth, and our work on the LCI and PSQ-QE a contribution to the development of measures for documenting qualitative change in the expressed meaning and significance of the life course experiences of young people.

Although the data presented here are preliminary, the findings provide evidence for the success of CLP in promoting positive qualitative change. Across both measures the basic pattern of qualitative change for participants in the CLP intervention condition tended to be positive, significant, and in the hypothesized direction relative to non-intervention controls. Although our preliminary results are qualified by indications that young people may respond differently to interventions, depending on their gender and their ethnicity, there are general trends of change that seem to be the result of our intervention. Specifically, the results document a relation between participation in CLP and short-term qualitative longitudinal change at the individual developmental level with respect to their life trajectories. With respect to the way they characterized their visions of themselves in the future, most youth initially portrayed Self-satisfying goals but tended to portray their future possible selves as realizing potentials (Self-actualizing) and/or or benefiting others (Altruistic) after intervention. Intervention also appeared to foster positive changes in identity (from negative and diffused toward self-assured and secure). Finally, and perhaps most importantly, intervention was also associated with the self-perception of a positive change in life course trajectory for many youth, who had sought our assistance in turning their lives around.

## REFERENCES

Catalano, R. F., Berglund, M. L., Ryan, J. A. M., Lonczak, H., & Hawkins, J. D. (1999). *Positive youth development in the United States: Research findings on evaluations of positive youth development programs.* Washington, DC: US Department of Health and Human Services.

Clausen, J. A. (1998). Life reviews and life stories. In J. Z. Giele & G. H. Elder (Eds.), *Methods of life course research: Qualitative and quantitative approaches* (pp. 189–212). Thousand Oaks, CA: Sage.

Elder, G. H. (1998). The life course and human development. In R. M. Lerner (Ed.), *Handbook of child psychology: Vol. 1. Theoretical models of human development.* New York: Wiley.

Erikson, E. H. (1968). *Identity: Youth and crisis.* New York: Norton.

Freire, P. (1970/1983). *Pedagogy of the oppressed.* New York: Herder & Herder.

Jensen, P., Hoagwood, K., & Trickett, E. (1999). Ivory towers or earthen trenches? Community collaborations to foster "real world" research. *Applied Developmental Science, 3*(4), 206–212.

Kurtines, W. M., Montgomery, M. J., Lewis Arango, L., & Kortsch, G. A. (2001, May). *Promoting positive youth development: Facilitating identity development in multi-problem adolescents.* Symposium presented at the Society for Research on Identity Formation, London, Ontario, Canada.

Lerner, R. M., Fisher, C. B., Weinberg, R. A. (2000). Toward a science for and of the people: Promoting civil society through the application of developmental science. *Child Development, 71*(1), 11–20.

Oyserman, D. (1987). *Possible selves and behavior: The case of juvenile delinquency.* Unpublished doctoral dissertation, University of Michigan, Ann Arbor.

Overton, W. (1998). Developmental psychology: Philosophy, concepts, and methodology. In R. M. Lerner (Ed.), W. Damon (Series Ed.), *Handbook of child psychology: Vol. 1. Theoretical models of human development* (5th ed., pp. 107–187). New York: Wiley.

Overton, W. F. (2003). Embodied development: Ending the nativism–empiricism debate. In C. Garcia Coll, E. Bearer, & R. Lerner (Eds.), *Nature and nurture: The complex interplay of genetic and environmental influences on human behavior and development* (pp. 201–223). Mahwah, NJ: Lawrence Erlbaum Associates, Inc.

EUROPEAN JOURNAL OF DEVELOPMENTAL PSYCHOLOGY, 2004, *1*(4), 399–411

# A dynamic systems perspective on social cognition, problematic behaviour, and intervention in adolescence

Anna Lichtwarck-Aschoff and Paul van Geert

*University of Groningen, The Netherlands*

In this article we discussed a dynamic systems view on social behaviour in adolescence. Social behaviour is defined as a self-organizing attractor landscape, based on a network of proximal (i.e., direct) causes. In some cases, social development is disturbed, leading to problematic behaviour in adolescence. The attractor landscape requires change and this change is achieved by therapy and intervention. Therapy and intervention are attempts to control complex, self-organizing systems, i.e., networks of proximal causes. We have noted that successful therapies and interventions do exactly that: change the network of proximal causes, within the rules and confinements of the contexts in which adolescent social behaviour occurs. Understanding the mechanism of such changes requires a different approach to studying and evaluating therapy and intervention, namely a focus on the various dynamics of individual trajectories.

Social cognition is the way people "… construct a relationship between themselves and the social objects of knowledge" (Barker & Newson, 1979). Social cognitions do not exist outside relations to other persons (Fogel, 1993; Bronfenbrenner, 1979; Valsiner & Connolly, 2003). Research on the development of social cognition, however, is mainly concerned with single, isolated individuals (Collins & Laursen, 1999).

Adolescence is a time of transition. Major changes take place in all domains of development (Petersen, Leffert, Graham, Alwin, & Ding, 1997; Halpern-Felsher, Millstein, & Irwin, 2002). Although in the majority of adolescents, social cognitive development occurs without any serious problems, there is also a significant group whose social cognitive development is disturbed. They need professional help in the form of intervention or therapy (Jackson & Bijstra, 2000).

Correspondence should be addressed to Anna Lichtwarck-Aschoff, University of Groningen, Grote kruisstraat 2/1, 9712 TS Groningen, The Netherlands.
E-mail: A.Lichtwarck@ppsw.rug.ne

http://www.tandf.co.uk/journals/pp/17405629.html    DOI: 10.1080/17405620444000157

In this article we will present a dynamic systems approach to problematic development in adolescence. We will first discuss the general framework, based on an example of (imaginary) problematic behaviour. We will then focus on intervention, therapy and effect evaluation.

## A DYNAMIC SYSTEMS APPROACH TO BEHAVIOUR, SOCIAL BEHAVIOUR AND SOCIAL COGNITION

### Edelweiss, edelweiss . . .

Jaap's hobby is mountaineering. When he is in the high Alps, he picks edelweiss. Edelweiss is a protected plant and Jaap has already been fined several times by the forestry officer. The fines are severe and each time it happens Jaap is pretty fed up with it. He stops climbing mountains for some time and confines himself to hiking in lower regions where the lure of edelweiss is lacking. But a real mountaineer like Jaap misses the challenge and it is never long before Jaap is again climbing the high mountains, finding himself in the unlawful possession of yet another edelweiss. The problem, at least in part, is that Jaap's girlfriend likes him to bring her edelweiss from the mountains, because she sees the fact that Jaap is willing to transgress the law just for the sake of giving her a flower as a proof of his love for her.

After a long talk with a friend, Jaap decides to follow an edelweiss aversion therapy course, where he learns to keep off the edelweiss and comparable protected species. But once he's in the mountains again, alone and in the flush of the climbing experience, Jaap cannot resist the temptation to pick edelweiss and is promptly arrested by a zealous Swiss forest officer. Finally, Jaap decides to quit mountaineering and to spend more time with his girlfriend. But Jaap is bored and misses the challenges and the edelweiss that bought him his girlfriend's admiration. Then Jaap learns about a friend who has a heavy motorbike for sale and Jaap now turns to a new and equally exciting pastime . . . .

What this story illustrates is that behaviour is a component of a complex and dynamic system. A dynamic system is a set of connected variables, i.e., changeable components that affect each other's states and properties. A dynamic system is characterized by relations of mutual determination: A affects B and vice versa. The state of any of the components is determined by the properties of the entire system, including the component itself. The entire system defines the resource limitations within which each of the components may vary (for more complete descriptions, see Thelen & Smith, 1994; Van Geert, 1994a, 2003).

## Network of forces

The specific behaviour of picking edelweiss, is subject to both positive (for instance, the admiration of his girlfriend) and negative influences (for instance, the heavy fines).

A metaphor that describes this aspect is the network metaphor or web of interacting components (see Figure 1). The components within a system are all mutually interconnected and influencing each other. Basic relationships consist of support, competition or conditionality (Van Geert, 1991, 1994a). The dynamics of support and competition that feature in a network are not a simple additive process where one factor cancels the other out.

Kunnen and Bosma (2000) modelled supportive and competitive relationships in a network of adolescent meaning making in interaction with a social context and stochastic experiences. Their growth model shows how the network of interactions between these components can produce various developmental patterns and trajectories.

## Attractor states

In the edelweiss example we saw that Jaap's behaviour was attracted to the pattern of edelweiss picking, given a number of conditions (being alone in

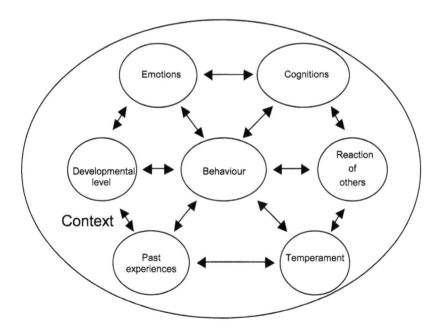

**Figure 1.** Example of a network.

the mountains, for instance). The dynamics of the situation are such that they drive the system into a state that is almost unavoidable and difficult to change. The structure of dynamic relationships in a network of interacting components leads to a limited number of such attractor states. Starting from some initial state, the system will move towards a self-reproducing state, i.e., a state producing a future state that is similar to itself. Attractors can also be processes, such as cycles of edelweiss picking and "good behaviour".

An attractor state is often depicted in the form of hills and valleys (see Figure 2) and is characterized by its depth, i.e., by its stability, which is the extent to which it resists attempts to change it.

The structure of attractor states is the attractor landscape. Attractor states can be inferred on the basis of a dynamic model of the network at issue (see for instance Steenbeek & Van Geert, 2004b). Given the dynamics of the network, it may be more or less easy to change the state of the system once an attractor state has been reached. If it is easy to do so, the system's attractor is shallow. Since a system is always subjected to (small) random events that exert weak influences on the system, a shallow attractor is characterized by a relatively high amount of (random) variation (like a ball in a shallow bowl that moves around as a consequence of small random influences, such as vibrations or puffs of air). If a considerable amount of effort is needed to move a system out of its state, the system's attractor is deep and there will be few spontaneous fluctuations. If a system has more than one attractor and if its present attractor state is shallow, relatively little effort is needed to move the system to a new attractor state. If the system has only one attractor or if the next available attractor occupies an entirely different region of the

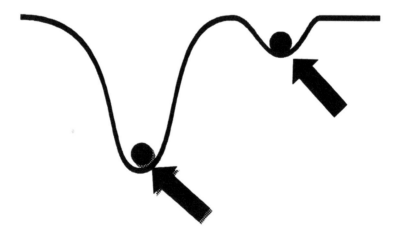

**Figure 2.** A system with a deep and a shallow attractor state; only little energy is needed to move it from the shallow into the deep attractor, from which it will probably not return, given the high amount of energy needed to get it out of the deep attractor.

system's state space, the system will almost always return to its original attractor state, irrespective of how deep or shallow this is.

## Causal structure: Proximal causes, context and distributed nature of causes

Mountain climbing creates the context for edelweiss picking, not only because edelweiss grows high up the mountain, but also because there are very few people on those high ridges and because the physical strains of mountain climbing create a flush that reduces Jaap's inhibitions. It is like a chain of small immediate causes that creates certain attractor states. The immediate or "proximal" causes exert a direct influence. There is no "distal" cause, such as a hypothetical underlying "craving-for-edelweiss". Smith, Thelen, Titzer, & McLin (1999) applied this idea to an infant's search for hidden objects. They showed that the infant's search is the temporal product of his interacting with contexts that offer specific affordances and constraints (an affordance is a particular property of the environment that, in combination with the abilities of the organism, attracts the organism towards a specific action; thus affordance and ability create a particular attractor state). The infant's behaviour is not governed by some underlying object concept that acts as an internal mechanism or behaviour-generating device. We do not intend to go as far as Smith et al. (1999) and discard the whole notion of concepts or knowledge. The notion of social cognition, for instance, is very useful in describing certain phenomena, as long as it is seen as referring to the actual dynamics of social interaction and not to some underlying mechanism in the person only. The proximal causes that explain social interaction are distributed over the whole network, e.g., over the participants of the social interaction (see for instance Mascolo & Margolis, this issue).

The framework of the *zone of proximal development*, i.e., the difference between the actual and the potential level of functioning (Vygotsky, 1978) applies very well to this idea. Van Geert (1994b, 1998) has argued that this principle is a major mechanism in any dynamic model of development, learning and change. A person's potential level is the level the person can achieve with the help of a more competent other person (an example of distributed causes). The potential level is a possible attractor state for the system. The actual level of a person is constantly changing as a consequence of his interiorizing the help given to him, causing the guiding person to continuously monitor and adjust his guidance and help.

The notion of behaviour as an attractor state of the entire system underlines another important feature of a complex dynamic system, namely the mutual dependency of subject and context. The context that is partly responsible for Jaap's edelweiss picking—being in the mountains—is not just an accidental external factor (an "independent variable"), it is in fact deliberately sought and created by Jaap's actions and the actions are determined by the self-created context (see Steenbeek & Van Geert, 2004a, 2004b, for an application to interaction in play).

The notions of contextual and proximal causes do not imply that the causes of problematic behaviour are in the context and not in the person. Rather, causes are distributed over the whole network, person and context included.

## Self organization and (non)linearity

The emergence of attractor states—such as the pattern of mountain climbing and edelweiss picking—is an example of a fundamental property of complex dynamic systems, namely self-organization. Self-organization is a very important principle for understanding developmental processes (Boker & Graham, 1998; Lewis & Granic, 2000; Port & Van Gelder, 1995; Van Geert, 1994a). Self-organization implies that the system moves towards a characteristic orderly attractor state that is not prescribed or pre-coded by some external component. A good example is childrearing. Parents have certain goals and ideas in mind about what to pass on to their children. However, these ideas are constantly changed by the reactions of their children. These small *real-time* interactions between parents and children shape the process and determine its direction (see for instance De Weerth, Van Geert, & Hoijtink, 1999; De Weerth & Van Geert, 2002) on idiosyncratic patterns of mother–child interaction; and Granic (2000) on the parent–child relation as a self-organizing system).

Self-organization is closely related to the principle of non-linearity. Since linear models play a major role in psychology, it is worthwhile discussing this issue in more detail.

Let us assume that we have a test for a person's propensity towards illegitimate flower picking (IFP) and a scale that specifies how inviting a context is with regard to IFP. Assuming that we have a record of the IFP of 500 respondents, it is not difficult to obtain a model for the sample, specifying the level of IFP (F) as a sum of a constant, a function of the personal propensity (P) towards IFP, a function of the level of contextual temptation (C) and, finally, an error component specifying the unexplained variance (*e*).

$$F = a + bP + cC + e$$

This is a linear model because it explains the flower picking as a sum of functions of predictors (Jackson, 1991). This linear model can be obtained because the data are conditionally independent, i.e., each flower-picking individual in the sample is independent of any other one.

However, in a dynamic model, the relationships are conditional and recursive, referring to a string or sequence of events. Let us assume Jaap has a relatively high propensity towards IFP (whatever form that may take). Given this propensity *and* Jaap's behavioural repertoire, it is likely that he will actively select an environment that highly facilitates the IFP. In this sequence, the environment is (partly) conditionally dependent on the propensity and the maintenance of the propensity is (partly) conditionally dependent on the environment. Given these conditional dependencies, it is impossible to specify "how much" of Jaap's IFP is due to his propensity and "how much" to the tempting environment.

The sequence contains stochastic events, such as the unexpected arrests by forest officers. If such an event occurs, it is likely that it will lead to Jaap's temporarily avoiding going to the mountains and thus, to a steep and sudden drop in his IFP. Hence, over time, Jaap's pattern of IFP looks like a highly non-linear, random-driven, saw-tooth pattern based on a dynamic of mutual interaction between the IFP propensity, the tempting environment and the fines.

The structure of a dynamic pattern is not necessarily similar to the way that this pattern is statistically distributed across the population, an issue that is related to the difference between intraindividual and interindividual variability (Molenaar, in press). Let us assume that Jaap's girl friend suffers from a moderate level of fear-of-heights (FoH; see Musher-Eizenman, Nesselroade, & Schmitz, 2002). Since Jaap takes her to the high Alps every year and to places that she experiences as vertiginous, we do an individual time-serial study of the association between FoH and exposure to vertiginous places. It is likely that, on a population level, this association is *negative*: the greater the FoH, the less likely it is that people will take high-mountain walks. However, let us assume that, in the case of Jaap's girl friend, exposure to high mountain paths temporarily increases her FoH, i.e., she will react with more fear as the number of vertigo experiences is increasing. Back in the lowlands, no longer exposed to cliffs, her FoH decreases. Within this particular process, the association is the opposite of that found on the population level: it is a *positive* association between FoH and the frequency of visiting vertiginous places. The gist of this example is that associations between variables on a group level (e.g., group evaluation of therapy) are not necessarily similar to those that hold on the level of individual processes (or therapies).

## A DYNAMIC SYSTEMS PERSPECTIVE ON INTERVENTION: PRINCIPLES AND EVALUATION

Social skills training is regarded as the most important tool to help youngsters with social problems (Bijstra & Nienhuis, 2003; Smith-Christopher, Nangle, & Hansen, 1993). However, different meta-studies yield different effect sizes, ranging from 0.19 to 0.78 (Magee-Quinn, Kavale,

Mathur, Rutherford, & Forness, 1999; Lösel & Beelmann, 2003; Ang & Hughes, 2002; Robinson, Smith, Miller, & Brownell, 1999; Stage & Quiroz, 1997). Some meta-studies found a negative outcome (Magee-Quinn et al., 1999; Robinson et al., 1999) while others pointed to the fact that social skills training in a group with only deviant peers can have adverse effects on the development of the children (Ang & Hughes, 2002; Dishion, McCord, & Poulin, 1999). Why does the same intervention have varying results for different individuals? In the following section we will try to answer this question by applying our dynamic systems perspective to intervention and to the evaluation of intervention effects.

## Intervention

Intervention starts off as an exogenous factor intended to influence the trajectory of the self-organizing system (Boker & Graham, 1998). Soon, the intervention becomes a part of the dynamic process, it becomes an endogenous part of the network of interconnected forces. For this reason, the results of an intervention are always dependent on the dynamics of the network in which they are incorporated. Therapy and intervention can be viewed as additional and temporary resource factors within the network composition.

The attractor metaphor helps us explain the inter-individual variability in intervention effects. Imagine a boy who has developed an aggressive communication style to resolve conflicts. The boy is now receiving therapy in order to change his aggressive style into a more appropriate communication style. To what extent this will be possible depends on the boy's attractor landscape. If the boy's aggressive behaviour is a very deep attractor, then a lot of "energy" (intervention, for instance) will be needed to move the behaviour away from this attractor and into another one. The presence of alternative attractors determines how easily the behaviour can change to a different state. The task of an intervention is to help create new attractors and deepen already existing ones.

However, behaviour is context-dependent: it is possible that the adolescent shows the desired behaviour in the context of the treatment but shifts back to the unwanted behaviour if he returns to the old peer environment. This happens if a different dynamic occurs in the treatment context compared to the peer context. A different context can contain very different causal factors resulting in different dynamics and attractor states. However, if a different context appeals to similar causal factors as the original context, it will contribute to the same dynamics as in the first, leading to similar attractor states.

In the overview of dynamic systems properties, we referred to the network as a system of competition and support relationships that co-operate to create characteristic attractor states. An application of this principle is the requirement that the context of the therapy is not in competition with other relevant contexts of the adolescent (school, family, etc.) concerning the behaviour that the therapy focuses on (Jackson & Bijstra, 2000). Behaviour rewarded in one context, for instance, must not be punished in a different context. Ideally, parents, school, peers and therapists should be working in concert.

Intervention attempts to change the network of proximal causal factors. Whether or not this goal succeeds depends on the nature of the causal process that leads to the unwanted attractor that the therapy tries to cure. If the process entails contextual factors that cannot be affected by the therapy, or if the personal causal factors are robust—for any reason—little effect will be obtained.

We have already mentioned the notion of proximal versus distal causes of behaviour and noted that dynamic systems self-organize on the basis of the network structure of proximal causes. Thus, we predict that treatments working on the network of proximal causes of behaviour will be the most effective. Ollendick and King (2004) give an overview of empirically supported treatments for children and adolescents. For ADHD, behavioural parent training and behaviour modification in the classroom are found to be effective. Children with ODD/CD showed the most improvement with behavioural parent training, functional family therapy and multi-systemic therapy. All these treatments are operating on the network system and are trying to change the whole composition, instead of the individual child alone. Additionally they are trying to change the proximal causes of the unwanted behaviour, which is a basic principle of behavioural therapy. In the case of adolescents, cognitions and interpretations must also be taken into account. This fact can probably explain why cognitive-behavioural therapies are efficacious (Ollendick & King, 2004).

Ollendick and King (2004) also discuss the case of manual-based treatments. The use of manuals seems to contradict the notion of self-organization. However, manuals can give structure to the complex system of intervention. By constraining the degrees of freedom of the complex therapeutic system, the manual helps the therapist to structure the network of interactions that must lead to a new attractor state, i.e., the desired therapeutic effect.

A manual can be compared with a teaching curriculum. The dynamics of teaching are compatible with the notion of the zone of proximal development, introduced earlier. In teaching, the curriculum helps structure the dynamics of teaching and learning, and defines the content of the potential level. The potential level is not a static entity, it is constantly changing, in order to find the best fit with the actual level of the adolescent, in the context of teaching as well as in the context of intervention and therapy.

The process of therapy and intervention boils down to the problem of control in a complex system. Mostly, a complex system, with its many levels, non-linear and self-organizational processes, cannot be controlled on basis of a linear model derived from statistical associations in a sample of independent cases. Controlling a complex system means that one must reckon with the fundamental features of complex systems. Things that work in one context will not work in another. Results of actions are not always unequivocal: results can be ambiguous, uncertain or vague (Rocha, 1997; Casti, 1995). These properties are intrinsic to the process of intervention in a complex system. Vagueness and fuzziness can be quantified, however, and used as indicators of the ongoing process (Van Geert & Van Dijk, 2003).

## Evaluation

In order to take adequate intervention decisions and avoid reverse effects, knowledge about the working mechanisms of a specific intervention is essential. According to Kazdin and Nock (2003) this knowledge is at present hardly available. They provide a number of recommendations for uncovering the mechanisms that make a therapy work, i.e., the causal factors that contribute to desired attractor states.

In accordance with our dynamic systems view, we believe that knowledge of the mechanisms requires observing individual interventions, on a proper time scale (comparable to *practice-based evidence*; Margison et al., 2000). A pre-test–post-test design will not reveal details about the operational mechanisms, because the chosen time scale is too coarse.

The fact that processes should be studied in terms of their individual dynamics is also supported by the evaluation of the *goodness-of-fit* (Singh & Oswald, 2004). It concerns the degree to which an intervention fits the patient along a range of other factors in addition to diagnosis. It is a systematic effort to answer the question "what is the most appropriate treatment approach for this specific problem in this particular patient at this present time?" A standardized measure for evaluations should assess the patient's goals and concerns, which are themselves important forces in the network of forces.

The importance of the entire network of forces in the dynamics of intervention is further emphasized by the difference between efficacy studies (regarding effects obtained in the research setting) and effectiveness studies (regarding effects obtained in the clinical setting) (Barrett & Ollendick, 2004). Although one can describe this difference technically as a problem of generalizability and external validity, the actual problem boils down to the question to what extent the dynamics of change are similar across different contexts.

Up till now, there have been few statistical methods available for studying longitudinal data sets from separate individuals, involving repeated measurements that run in the order of tens instead of hundreds. However, the recent increase in statistical simulation methods applicable to small time series samples may provide better possibilities for the future (Van Geert & Van Dijk, 2002; Todman & Dugard, 2001).

The meta-studies about effectiveness of social skills trainings are all done in accordance with the traditional random control group design. This design is based on a statistical comparison of scores of different groups (Liebert & Liebert, 1995) and is recommended as the most suitable method (Phares & Trull, 1997; Gray, 1999; Remschmidt, 2001). In our view, this recommendation is not warranted. One's method of research depends on the question one wants to answer and this question is itself part of a particular dynamic. Take for instance the perspective—and associated dynamics—of policy makers, where the classical experimental design can be a useful tool. The experimental design compares groups and provides information that a policy maker can use to distribute scarce financial means over those groups. However, even here the experimental design has its limitations if it is only used to focus on average gains. Assume that an intervention program is successful in reducing overall aggression in a school but does not succeed in avoiding exceptional events, such as a student bringing in a fire arm and killing a teacher. In that case, the public opinion might blame the school for having failed in its attempts to treat aggression. However, the dynamics of such extreme events are probably very different from the dynamics that lead to aggression that falls under the possibilities of a standard intervention program.

# REFERENCES

Ang, R. P., & Hughes, J. N. (2002). Differential benefits of skills training with antisocial youth based on group composition: A meta-analytic investigation. *School Psychology Review, 31,* 164–185.

Barker, W., & Newson, L. (1979). The development of social cognition: Definition and location. In S. Mogdil & C. Mogdil (Eds.), *Toward a theory of psychological development.* Windsor, UK: NFER.

Barrett, P. M., & Ollendick, T. H. (2004). *Handbook of interventions that work with children and adolescents: Prevention and treatment.* New York: Wiley.

Bijstra, J., & Nienhuis, B. (2003). Sociale-vaardigheidstrainingen. Meten we of meten we niet? *De Psycholoog, 38,* 174–178.

Boker, S. M., & Graham, J. (1998). A dynamical systems analysis of adolescent substance abuse. *Multivariate Behavioural Research, 33,* 479–507.

Bronfenbrenner, U. (1979). *The ecology of human development. experiment by nature and design.* Cambridge, MA: Harvard University Press.

Casti, J. L. (1995). *Complexification: Explaining a paradoxical world through the science of surprise.* New York: Harper Perennial.

Collins, W. A. E., & Laursen, B. E. (1999). *Relationships as developmental contexts* (14th ed.). Mahwah, NJ: Lawrence Erlbaum Associates, Inc.

De Weerth, C., & Van Geert, P. (2002). Changing patterns of infant behaviour and mother–infant interaction: Intra- and inter-individual variability. *Infant Behaviour and Development*, *24*(4), 347–371.

De Weerth, C., Van Geert, P., & Hoijtink, H. (1999). Intra-individual variability in infant behaviour. *Developmental Psychology*, *35*(4), 1102–1112.

Dishion, T. J., McCord, J., & Poulin, F. (1999). When interventions harm: Peer groups and problem behaviour. *American psychologist*, *54*, 755–764.

Fogel, A. (1993). *Developing through relationships: Origins of communication, self, and culture* (8th ed.). Chicago, IL: University of Chicago Press.

Granic, I. (2000). The self-organization of parent–child relations: Beyond bidirectional models. In M. D. Lewis & I. Granic (Eds.), *Emotion, development, and self-organization* (pp. 267–298). Cambridge, UK: Cambridge University Press.

Gray, P. (1999). *Psychology*. New York: Worth Publishers.

Halpern-Felsher, B. L., Millstein, S. G., & Irwin, C. E. J. (2002). Work group II: Healthy adolescent psychosocial development. *Journal of Adolescent Health*, *31*, 201–207.

Jackson, E. A. (1991). *Perspectives of nonlinear dynamics* (Vol. 1). Cambridge, UK: Cambridge University Press.

Jackson, S. (A. E.), & Bijstra, J. (2000). Overcoming psychosocial difficulties in adolescence: Toward the development of social competence. *European Review of Applied Psychology*, *50*, 267–274.

Kazdin, A. E., & Nock, M. K. (2003). Delineating mechanisms of change in child and adolescent therapy: Methodological issues and research recommendations. *Journal of Child Psychology and Psychiatry and Allied Disciplines*, *44*, 1116–1129.

Kunnen, E. S., & Bosma, H. A. (2000). The development of meaning making: A dynamic systems approach. *New Ideas in Psychology*, *18*, 57–82.

Lewis, M. D., & Granic, I. (2000). *Emotion, development, and self-organization. Dynamic systems approaches to emotional development*. Cambridge, UK: Cambridge University Press.

Liebert, R. M., & Liebert, L. L. (1995). *Science and behaviour. An introduction to methods of psychological research*. New Jersey: Prentice Hall.

Lösel, F., & Beelmann, A. (2003). Effects of child skills training in preventing antisocial behaviour: A systematic review of randomized evaluations. *Annals of the American Academy of Political and Social Science*, *587*, 84–109.

Magee-Quinn, M., Kavale, K. A., Mathur, S. R., Rutherford, R. B. J., & Forness, S. R. (1999). A meta-analysis of social skill interventions for students with emotional or behavioural disorders. *Journal of Emotional and Behavioural Disorders*, *7*, 54–64.

Margison, F. R., Barkham, M., Evans, C., McGrath, G., Clark, J. M., Audin, K., & Connell, J. (2000). Measurement and psychotherapy: Evidence-based practice and practice-based evidence. *British Journal of Psychiatry*, *177*, 123–130.

Molenaar, P. (in press). A manifesto on psychology as idiographic science: Bringing the person back into the scientific psychology—this time for ever. *Measurement*.

Musher-Eizenman, D. R., Nesselroade, J. R., & Schmitz, B. (2002). Perceived control and academic performance: A comparison of high- and low-performing children on within-person change-patterns. *International Journal of Behavioural Development*, *26*, 540–547.

Ollendick, T. H., & King, N. J. (2004). Empirically supported treatments for children and adolescents: Advances toward evidence-based practice. In P. M. Barrett & T. H. Ollendick (Eds.), *Handbook of interventions that work with children and adolescents: Prevention and treatment*. Chichester, UK: Wiley.

Petersen, A. C., Leffert, W., Graham, B., Alwin, J., & Ding, S. (1997). Promoting mental health during the transition into adolescence. In J. E. Schulenberg, J. L. E. Maggs, & K. E. Hurrelmann (Eds.), *Health risks and developmental transitions during adolescence*. Cambridge, UK: Cambridge University Press.

Phares, E. J., & Trull, T. J. (1997). *Clinical psychology.* Pacific Grove, CA: Brooks/Cole Publishing Company.

Port, R. F., & Van Gelder, T. (1995). *Mind as motion: Explorations in the dynamics of cognition.* Cambridge, MA: Bradford Books/MIT Press.

Remschmidt, H. (2001). *Psychotherapy with children and adolescents.* Cambridge, UK: Cambridge University Press.

Robinson, T. R., Smith, S. W., Miller, M. D., & Brownell, M. T. (1999). Cognitive behaviour modification of hyperactivity-impulsivity and aggression: A meta-analysis of school-based studies. *Journal of Educational Psychology, 91,* 195–203.

Rocha, L. M. (1997). *Evidence sets and contextual genetic algorithms: Exploring uncertainty, context, and embodiment in cognitive and biological systems.* Doctoral dissertation, New York: Binghamton University.

Singh, N. N., & Oswald, D. P. (2004). Evaluation issues in evidence-based practice. In P. M. Barrett & T. H. Ollendick (Eds.), *Handbook of interventions that work with children and adolescents. Prevention and treatment.* Chichester, UK: Wiley.

Smith-Christopher, J., Nangle, D. W., & Hansen, D. J. (1993). Social skills interventions with adolescents: Current issues and procedures. *Behaviour Modification, 17,* 314–338.

Smith, L. B., Thelen, E., Titzer, R., & McLin, D. (1999). Knowing in the context of acting: The task dynamics of the A-not-B error. *Psychological Review, 106,* 235–260.

Stage, S. A., & Quiroz, D. R. (1997). A meta-analysis of interventions to decrease disruptive classroom behaviour in public education settings. *School Psychology Review, 26,* 333–368.

Steenbeek, H. W., & Van Geert, P. (2004a). A dynamic systems model of dyadic play interaction in children. *Manuscript in preparation.*

Steenbeek, H. W., & Van Geert, P. L. C. (2004b). *Emotional expression and behaviour in dyadic play in children of different sociometric statuses: A dynamic systems approach.* Manuscript submitted for publication.

Thelen, E., & Smith, L. B. (1994). *A dynamic systems approach to the development of cognition and action* (23rd ed.). Cambridge, MA: MIT Press.

Todman, J. B., & Dugard, P. (2001). Single-case and small-*n* experimental designs: A practical guide to randomization tests. Mahwah, NJ: Lawrence Erlbaum Associates, Inc.

Valsiner, J., & Connolly, K. (2003). *Developmental psychology.* London: Sage.

Van Geert, P., & Van Dijk, M. (2002). Focus on variability: New tools to study intra-individual variability in developmental data. *Infant Behaviour & Development, 151,* 1–35

Van Geert, P. L. C., & Van Dijk, M. (2003). The problem of inter-observer reliability in ambiguous observation data. *First Language, 23*(3), 259–284.

Van Geert, P. L. C. (1991). A dynamic systems model of cognitive and language growth. *Psychological Review, 98,* 3–53.

Van Geert, P. L. C. (1994a). *Dynamic systems of development: Change between complexity and chaos.* New York: Prentice Hall/Harvester Wheatsheaf.

Van Geert, P. L. C. (1994b), Vygotskian dynamics of development. *Human Development, 37,* 346–365.

Van Geert, P. L. C. (1998). A dynamic systems model of basic developmental mechanisms: Piaget, Vygotsky and beyond. *Psychological Review, 105*(4), 634–677.

Van Geert, P. L. C. (2003). Dynamic systems approaches and modelling of developmental processes. In J. Valsiner & K. J. Conoly (Eds.), *Handbook of developmental psychology* (pp. 640–672). London: Sage.

Vygotsky, L. (1978). *Mind in society: The development of higher psychological processes.* Cambridge, MA: Harvard University Press.

# SUBJECT INDEX

www.ingramcontent.com/pod-product-compliance
Ingram Content Group UK Ltd.
Pitfield, Milton Keynes, MK11 3LW, UK
UKHW020348010325
455677UK00021B/342